There is a critical need for leadership to enable organizations to harmonize financial, social, and environmental requirements. *Purpose-driven Innovation Leadership for Sustainable Development* offers fascinating insights into a senior leadership team's efforts to find balance among divergent requirements and logics in the context of a rapidly growing 'for-purpose enterprise'. Through a detailed, ethnographic case study the readers are presented with general principles that can be applied in many contemporary organisations to help with navigating the unavoidable tensions that derive from the pursuit of innovation and the attempt to reconcile multiple objectives. The result is an evidence-based informative and practical guide for anyone interested in exploring how to better lead for impact.

Dr Marco Berti, *Associate Professor of Management and Organizations, Nova School of Business & Economics, Lisbon*

Purpose-driven Innovation Leadership for Sustainable Development takes a bold approach to a relatively new field of study. The research explores how the dynamics of competing strategic purpose-driven growth demands can manifest in a senior leadership team. Paradoxical tensions identified included those between the need to pursue both breakthrough innovation and incremental innovation, along with the need to pursue both purpose and profit. By taking the reader through a rich case study methodology, the book bridges the common gap between in-depth qualitative research and practical actionable insights and applications.

Professor Eric Knight, *Professor of Strategic Management at Macquarie Business School, New South Wales, Australia*

Purpose-driven Innovation Leadership for Sustainable Development

Purpose-driven Innovation Leadership for Sustainable Development presents invaluable insights into how leaders can balance competing innovation demands. The book reports on research from an in-depth case study, which reveals the importance of developing highly adaptive and innovative responses through periods of rapid growth – while simultaneously ensuring organisational stability grounded in a clear core purpose. 'Paradox' theory is introduced as a constructive theoretical lens for exploring these complexities of leadership sensemaking in innovation contexts. The findings demonstrate how to incorporate both perspectives to establish a robust innovation culture.

This book aims to equip readers with evidence-based principles that can be readily applied in practice. The qualitative methodology, which includes case studies and interviews conducted with global innovation leaders, uncovers powerful strategies from relevant real-world experiences. Targeted 'Reflection and Action' questions are also included to guide implementation.

Purpose-driven Innovation Leadership for Sustainable Development will support researchers, educators, and students in the higher education sector who would like to investigate contemporary innovation leadership principles and practices. The book will also interest business leaders hoping to access rigorous research studies on the topic presented in an effective actionable format.

Gaia Grant is a researcher and lecturer at the University of Sydney Business School and the Executive Director of Tirian International Consultancy. In her research, Gaia has focused on how leaders can create a culture that supports sustainable and responsible innovation – along with exploring creative thinking and innovative problem-solving strategies to deal with wicked problems. Gaia has facilitated practical innovation solutions for a range of organisations globally, from Fortune 500 companies to not-for-profits, utilising the unique 'Innovative Change Leader Inventory' (iCLi) and 'Dynamic Polar Positioning' (DPoP) tools she has developed from her research.

Routledge Focus on Business and Management

The fields of business and management have grown exponentially as areas of research and education. This growth presents challenges for readers trying to keep up with the latest important insights. *Routledge Focus on Business and Management* presents small books on big topics and how they intersect with the world of business research.

Individually, each title in the series provides coverage of a key academic topic, whilst collectively the series forms a comprehensive collection across the business disciplines.

Leadership and Strategic Management
Decision-Making in Times of Change
Paolo Boccardelli and Federica Brunetta

Artificial Intelligence and Project Management
An Integrated Approach to Knowledge-Based Evaluation
Tadeusz A. Grzeszczyk

Organizational Aesthetics
Artful Visual Representations of Business and Organizations
Barbara Fryzel and Aleksander Marcinkowski

Open Strategy for Digital Business
Managing in ICT-Driven Environments
Ewa Lechman, Joanna Radomska and Ewa Stańczyk-Hugiet

Purpose-driven Innovation Leadership for Sustainable Development
A Qualitative Case Study Approach
Gaia Grant

For more information about this series, please visit: www.routledge.com/Routledge-Focus-on-Business-and-Management/book-series/FBM

Purpose-driven Innovation Leadership for Sustainable Development
A Qualitative Case Study Approach

Gaia Grant

Routledge
Taylor & Francis Group

NEW YORK AND LONDON

First published 2024
by Routledge
605 Third Avenue, New York, NY 10158

and by Routledge
4 Park Square, Milton Park, Abingdon, Oxon, OX14 4RN

Routledge is an imprint of the Taylor & Francis Group, an informa business

Library of Congress Cataloging-in-Publication Data
Names: Grant, Gaia, author.
Title: Purpose-driven innovation leadership for sustainable development :
a qualitative case study approach / Gaia Grant.
Description: New York, NY : Routledge, 2025. |
Series: Routledge focus on business and management | Includes
bibliographical references and index.
Identifiers: LCCN 2024016545 | ISBN 9781032730219 (hardback) |
ISBN 9781032731025 (paperback) | ISBN 9781003426691 (ebook)
Subjects: LCSH: Sustainable development—Management. | Technological
innovations—Environmental aspects—Management. | Leadership.
Classification: LCC HD75.6 .G734 2025 | DDC 658.4/08—dc23/
eng/20240419
LC record available at https://lccn.loc.gov/2024016545

ISBN: 978-1-032-73021-9 (hbk)
ISBN: 978-1-032-73102-5 (pbk)
ISBN: 978-1-003-42669-1 (ebk)

DOI: 10.4324/9781003426691

Typeset in Times New Roman
by codeMantra

Contents

viii *Contents*

Figures

Tables

Tables

1 Introduction
The motivation and rationale behind this research

I have long believed that innovation can and should be life changing. Close to 30 years of consulting work with a range of organisations from not-for-profits through to government organisations and Fortune 500 companies initially led me to this view. We should be able to solve the world's most challenging or wicked problems through skilfully applied imagination and innovation implementation. So why do we often struggle to do this well?

My initial forays into exploring this topic identified that we are not necessarily held back by developments in technology. Technology has already reached the point where we can utilise generative artificial intelligence, build semiautonomous vehicles, fight disease through nanotechnology and experiment with creating new ecosystems on Mars. The main obstacles are now typically the human factors. Some of these factors can include resistance to change, complex ethical considerations such as the role of AI and tensions between different strategic approaches. At the core of these, I have found, are tensions arising from competing pressures that are increasingly complex and difficult to navigate.

I developed an interest in exploring what is driving these sorts of challenges and how we can deal with them better. This led me to conduct research case studies to delve deeper, and beyond the superficial 'sound bite' approach of picking up on key innovation phrases and trends, as often happens in business. I wanted to identify the rich complexities of what can happen at an individual and organisational level to block or challenge the innovation process, along with identifying what leadership dynamics might foster purpose-driven innovation more effectively.

To this end, I share here a study I conducted with leaders of a highly innovative not-for-profit/social enterprise as a profound illustration of how it is possible to navigate purpose-driven innovation. I have also included other examples from companies I have worked with in a consulting capacity over the years.

This book takes a rigorous and scholarly approach to provide details of the process of how the data was collected and analysed. I felt that this format was appropriate for an in-depth case study to help provide more

DOI: 10.4324/9781003426691-1

background and context than might otherwise be afforded in a more standard academic journal article. The intent was not only to take readers on a journey into the research process to share the rigorous methodological approach taken but also to identify really clear and accessible connections with insights related to principles and practices that can be easily implemented in business contexts.

My recent research into innovation leadership has confirmed what I have long suspected. It can be incredibly difficult to resolve the tensions related to competing demands from complex rapid-change contexts – particularly for leaders of for-purpose organisations – and this can impede the innovation process. Through this series of studies, I therefore sought to understand how it is possible to manage these innovation tensions.

My hope is that overall the approach I have taken will be beneficial for a wide range of readers. First and foremost, it should be of interest to academic scholars who would gain value from reading about the theoretical and methodological approaches and how these led to the findings. The book will also be a useful resource for educators in the higher education sector as a text, as it includes a step-by-step guide to the research process and discussion questions. Additionally, it should also be of general interest to university students, who would benefit from gleaning the insights and applications that will prepare them for their work in the business context as well as learning about the value of an in-depth qualitative research process. And finally, the book should be beneficial for business leaders and innovators wanting to ensure they draw on evidence-based research results, as they will be able to refer to this study for inspiration and guidance.

Why is innovation leadership so challenging?

Innovation is now seen as a priority by most organisations. It is recognised as an imperative for both survival and strategic advantage in a rapid change and hypercompetitive environment.[1] Numerous academic studies as well as business rankings and indices have highlighted the importance of innovation, and the concept has now become so widely used that it has been labelled in popular media as 'the buzzword of the decade'.[2]

Innovation is the most important determinant of organisation performance overall,[3] and senior executives believe it is critical for economic performance, identifying innovation as one of their top three strategic priorities.[4] Ironically although rapid-change environments require strategic leadership for innovation to ensure survival,[5] these environments produce ambiguities from competing demands which generate unique tensions for leaders.[6] These tensions, in turn, often subvert the leader's endeavours to sustain successful innovation.[7]

At the core of these competing demands is the imperative of keeping up with the pace of change – which requires agile adaptation for rapid innovation – along with simultaneously ensuring responsible and reliable performance.[8] The tensions from apparently contradictory requirements such as these can appear to be irreconcilable.[9] Related competing demands and the associated tensions identified in leading for innovation have included the need to: explore breakthrough new innovation opportunities while maintaining current systems and structures;[10] both generate and implement new ideas;[11] allow for diversity and adaptability along with ensuring stability;[12] innovation plan for the future while focusing on survival in the present;[13] and enable centralisation along with decentralisation.[14] Scholars now recognise the ambiguities and complexities of leading for innovation and the need to deal with the competing innovation demands simultaneously.[15] Further research in this area will be of critical importance for ensuring innovation leadership for a sustainable future.

Research on innovation has predominantly focused on organisation innovation and entrepreneurship,[16] and connections to *organisation leadership* in the innovation context have not been as clear.[17] Although the number of research articles on innovation increased from around 50 per year in 1981 to more than 340,000 per year in 2023, firm-level innovation processes remained the focus of more than 50% of these articles. The critical role of organisational leadership for innovation has now become a key area of interest.[18] Clear links between leadership and innovation have been established, with some theorists identifying leadership as having the greatest impact on innovation.[19] A number of studies now confirm the role of leadership as one of the most significant precursors to innovation,[20] particularly at the senior leadership level.[21]

While there is a growing recognition of the need for leaders to simultaneously pursue such contradictory goals for more sustainable development,[22] *how* this can be achieved effectively is not yet well understood. Little is known about the dynamics of how leaders and leadership teams experience and respond to the tensions from complex competing innovation demands in for-purpose organisations. Insights into these experiences and responses can further our knowledge of how senior leaders can address competing innovation demands.

To clarify the definitions of the keywords, in this book we will explore:

- **Innovation.** Novel and useful developments that challenge and move beyond current parameters to create a new value.
- **Purpose-driven innovation.** Strategic developments designed to build new opportunities in line with an organisation's core principles.
- **Senior Leadership.** The CEO and direct reports.
- **Sustainable development.** Practical developmental changes that improve people's lives and the planet, and that can be maintained over time.

Tapping into leadership tensions makes it possible to identify core challenge areas and opportunities for positive sustainable change.

Motivation and preparation for the research

I became particularly interested in exploring the impact of tensions from competing demands in innovation contexts after observing the effect on client organisations. My experience as a practitioner in the field of management consulting had revealed how these tensions could threaten to fragment an organisation if not managed effectively.

I could see the impact on not-for-profit and social enterprise organisations that had been established to serve a social purpose. I identified they had to face multiple competing demands. Informal discussions with senior leaders from these organisations revealed that although a number of them were planning to be innovative in their desire to best fulfil the organisation's mission, their attempts to achieve these goals were often thwarted by the tensions.

When considering these challenges, I recognised that it would be beneficial to understand the dynamics behind the senior leader experience to assist them with knowing how to identify and address the tensions. I also anticipated that the insights gained might inform the development of an instrument that could provide feedback for leaders when dealing with these challenges. At this point, I realised it would be therefore important to explore both the theoretical propositions from the research to support further development in the area along with the applicable practical implications.

My involvement with one particular organisation during the early phases of the study confirmed the potential importance of this research. I outline my observations of this organisation in detail here to provide an insight into some initial experiences that eventually shaped the formal research approach and design.

This organisation had been set up to assist rural communities in impoverished regions in Asia through developing more innovative farming techniques. The organisation had been established with government funding, but the strategic goal was to shift to a financially self-sustaining social enterprise model through partnering with local businesses. I had worked with the organisation over a period of three years soon after it was established. During this time, it was evident that despite the impressive business approach and dedicated team, there was an internal struggle to resolve the increasing tensions.

As the organisation grew to over 140 employees, cracks began to show. Retention was starting to become an issue, and staff surveys revealed that employees were becoming disillusioned and disengaged. Rather than erupting as overt conflicts, these tensions were frequently simmering below the surface, often undetected by those who might be able to address them. I had been called in by the general manager to assist with working on the organisation leadership and culture, and specifically to support the employees to generate more creative solutions in their work. It soon became clear, however, that there was a culture of fear that was negatively impacting innovation confidence and capabilities.

I identified that my work with this international not-for-profit organisation could provide some insights into the challenges for senior leaders in
this context, so I decided to use the opportunity to help inform the research
design while the main research project started taking shape. After gaining
ethics approval, I asked the general manager for permission to collect qualitative data (through observations and interviews) that might help to identify
the core issues and provide diagnostic information. I interviewed a range of
employees from different levels in the organisation to get a feel for their experiences and concerns. I also had the opportunity to observe these people at
work in the office, including observing the senior leadership team in their
weekly meetings.

Several employees were reluctant to say too much in the interviews,
and others found it difficult articulating the challenges, so I decided to use
a 'draw and talk' technique to see if I could access the deeper issues.[23] This
involved asking the interviewees to draw pictures representing the concepts
they discussed. The drawings produced in this exercise led to some particularly fascinating insights. As an example, when I asked how individuals saw
the leadership team, the general manager drew a picture of rough pieces of
a puzzle coming together to form the shape of a holistic sphere, saying that
he believed the team was 'collaborative' and 'equal-minded' and 'coming
together well'. Another member of the organisation drew a picture of a large
boot with the label 'boss' on it. This employee explained how his picture had
all the staff represented as 'worker ants' running around on the ground in
panic or trying to climb onto the boss's boot. When asked where he was in the
picture, this individual pointed to an ant on the toe of the boot in impending
danger of getting squashed underneath it, as the boot was suspended in prepa-
ration to take the next step. He explained that he felt the fear of imminent
ruthless destruction.

Observations of the executive meetings provided further confirmation that
a fear of the general manager was impacting the culture. At all levels. During these meetings, the general manager often sat in a corner of the room
with his arms crossed and he would shut down new ideas with comments
like 'We've done that before', 'There isn't a budget for that' or 'We don't
have time for that'. This confirmed indications from a number of sources that
while the general manager had believed he was providing an open environment for innovation, a focus on metrics and results along with an abrupt management style was leading to tensions that stifled the opportunity to achieve
the desired innovation results. At the same time, through these actions, the
general manager was inadvertently threatening the stability and sustainability
of the organisation.

The observations of this organisation, along with many others from my
years of consulting work, supported my perceptions that senior leaders and
senior leadership teams are in a critical position to influence sustainable innovation and growth. The observations reinforced my initial impressions that it

would be useful to identify a means of better understanding the for-purpose innovation tensions in organisations at the senior leadership level. This would assist with providing useful practical feedback for these leaders.

The development of the key research question

With my interest piqued and some early emergent concepts as a starting point, I consulted the literature to identify how this research could build on previous work in the field.

A review of the literature determined that the key focus areas should include an understanding of the nature of competing innovation demands in complex rapid change contexts, with an emphasis on understanding how senior leaders experience and make sense of these demands, particularly in for-purpose organisations. I also determined that 'paradox' could provide a valuable theoretical lens for understanding how senior leaders make sense of the competing demands. Figure 1.1 illustrates the focal areas of the research, delineating the points of convergence and integration between the various intersecting fields and demonstrating the relationship to the overarching research aim.

With the context in mind, I found that several studies in the literature supported observations that the complexity of contemporary environments often requires these senior leaders to deal with multiple competing strategic demands simultaneously.[24] Further, unique polarising demands and associated tensions related to leadership in innovation contexts have been identified.[25] The literature refers to the need for a focus on breakthrough innovation through *exploration* to meet the demands

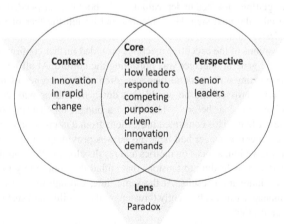

Figure 1.1 Focus areas for research

of the contemporary rapid change context, acknowledging that this focus can threaten the organisation's stability. Equally important, therefore, is the need for incremental innovation through the *exploitation* of current systems and products which can provide a more stable foundation for growth, also acknowledging that an overemphasis on stability as a trade-off can reduce competitiveness and survival in a rapid change context.[26]

After considering the best perspective to take, I identified that the tensions from these competing demands are often experienced most acutely by senior leaders, as they are responsible for the strategic development of the organisation.[27] Senior leaders account for about 5–20% of variance in company financial performance[28] and are recognised as the 'core drivers of sustainable development',[29] so it is critical to understand the nature and impact of these tensions at this level. Not only do senior leaders support the types of group interaction that enable and guide innovative processes in their teams,[30] they are also able to create the conditions required for innovation implementation.[31] These leaders use a number of managerial levers to directly and indirectly impact innovation,[32] including strategic missions and goals, resource allocation, organisational learning and management tools, and culture, which work together to support innovation direction and maintenance.[33]

The theoretical lens of paradox was utilised to investigate the underlying tensions from a range of competing demands that emerge as organisations innovate and grow, and to explain how these tensions can manifest and be addressed.[34] Paradoxical tensions are defined as 'contradictory yet interrelated',[35] along with 'synergistic and persistent'.[36] The basic assumption is that at the heart of the tensions that arise from competing demands are paradoxes which, if identified and managed effectively, can support or even fuel sustainable innovation and growth.[37]

It has been established that there needs to be more research into how senior leaders navigate these paradoxical competing demands, as many senior leaders are unaware of the underlying tensions and how these tensions influence their actions.[38]

The methodological approach was designed to complement this research focus. The methodology included, firstly, a series of interviews with senior leaders from a range of organisations to gain insight into their cognitive frames, as these can be identified through leaders' words and actions.[39] The initial interviews revealed that these leaders usually strategise for innovation and make innovation-related decisions in a range of contexts, including in naturally occurring teams. My observations of the agricultural organisation in Asia, as described in detail earlier, had also highlighted the importance of the team context.

I determined it would therefore be important to analyse senior team experiences in situ across these different levels. This led to an in-depth case study, which provided the opportunity to observe what individual leaders bring to the team, and how they negotiate differences to reach consensus. I established that exploring how individual senior leaders negotiate their own orientations in relation to other team members would be important as well as identifying how the senior leadership team as a whole agrees to move forward.[40] I came to appreciate that this could lead to a better understanding of how an intersubjective world is created and maintained.[41] This process involved investigating how a shared sense of meaning is negotiated[42] and how coordinated action between senior leaders is facilitated.[43]

The core research question addressed in the program was therefore:

> *How do senior leaders experience and respond to competing purpose-driven innovation demands?*

Levels of analysis

The studies incorporated in this research were designed to focus on different levels of analysis. I expected that this would provide relevant frameworks for exploring senior leadership experiences in complex innovation contexts.[44]

As senior leaders must typically operate at a number of levels simultaneously, the focus on different levels was identified as appropriate for analysing senior leadership practices in context.[45] Senior leaders will usually experience and make sense of strategic requirements at the individual, team and organisation levels,[46] and it is recognised that more research at these different levels of analysis needs to be conducted.[47] The emphasis in this research was on the naturally occurring leadership formations in which senior leaders are commonly required to operate.

The first level of focus was the individual senior leader level, as individual leaders have individual cognitive approaches and mindsets which impact the outcomes of actions at all levels of the organisation. Early exploratory work therefore established the importance of gathering data from a range of individual senior leaders through interviews.

The second area of focus was on senior leadership teams. I decided to explore senior leader experiences in a case organisation context after it was identified that an intensive case study would provide the opportunity for in-depth exploration and analysis. Early ethnographic observations of senior leaders in this case study showed that understanding how senior leaders operate in senior leadership teams is important, as these teams are the most common working units. An emergent phenomenon of interest thus became how leaders with their own individual orientations come together as a team to navigate competing innovation demands.

After observing the senior leadership team in the case organisation for a short period of time, it soon also became apparent that the full team comprised a highly significant and powerful sub-team – a senior leadership duo. The dynamics of this sub-unit and the impact on the whole senior leadership team then emerged as a third area of focus for the research program.

Methodological overview

The core of this research involved a process-oriented approach. This approach enabled the identification of the dynamic interconnections between people, situations and events,[48] and established the need for an emergent design.[49] The integrated research program that was shaped through this process incorporated the different levels of analysis and complementary methodologies to identify unique phenomena. An outline of the emergent integrated program design is illustrated in Figure 1.2.

Senior leadership individual level: general interviews

The first part of the research program focused on identifying the experiences of individual senior leaders. This involved conducting inductive qualitative interviews with senior leaders responsible for innovation in their organisation and with a focus on purpose-driven innovation.

In this phase, I interviewed 68 leaders from a range of organisations including Finance (10), Manufacturing (7), Education (7), Government (6), Consulting (6), IT (5), Pharmaceutical (3), Media (3), Food and beverage (2), Telecommunications (1), Transport (1), Medical (1), Hospitality (1), Service (1) and Not-for-Profit (14). The headquarters of these companies were located throughout Asia Pacific (43), North America (21) and Europe (4). The organisations ranged in size from small (up to 50 employees) (21), to medium (up to 1000 employees and over $10 million turnover) (19), and large (1000+ employees and up to billions of dollars in revenue) (28). The leaders' role

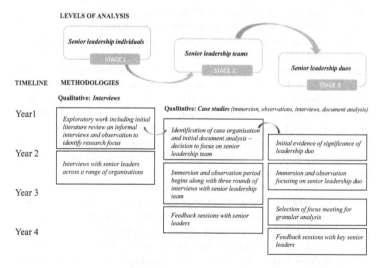

Figure 1.2 Integrated research program developed over the research period

titles included C-suite and board members (10), executive directors (32), innovation leaders (19), sustainability leaders (9) and innovation consultants and researchers (9).

Relevant insights from these interviews have been included in pull-out text boxes throughout the book to provide additional perspectives on the findings from the core case study.

The literature on ambidextrous leadership, which relates to identifying paradoxical leadership approaches in innovation contexts,[50] initially provided a guide for understanding and framing the emergent elements. The analysis of the interview data helped to identify additional individual micro-level factors that may impact how senior leaders strategise in the context of purpose-driven innovation.

Senior leadership team and duo levels: case study

As the number of interviews reached a natural saturation point,[51] the value of conducting an in-depth case study to observe senior leaders in situ became apparent. A case organisation was then selected for a more intensive focus. The main part of research program therefore transitioned into the intensive case study.

In this book I refer to the case study organisation as 'Social Support Services' (SSO). The research into this enterprise involved observations of an intact senior leadership team in their naturally occurring contexts, along with observations of the core senior leadership duo within the team. The focus at the senior team level was on studying the senior leadership team over an 18-month period in a longitudinal ethnographic case study to ensure there was the opportunity to investigate the emergent phenomena in granular detail.

The case organisation was a highly innovative and rapidly growing not-for-profit working with vulnerable migrants and refugees, and I knew from stories in the media that there had been significant challenges for the senior leaders related to how to innovate sustainably and responsibly. I planned to conduct immersive case study research with this organisation, and to spend time as a participant observer over an 18-month period where possible, observing regular formal and informal senior leadership meetings and interactions. Through this process, I was able to identify responses to tensions arising from the competing demands of innovation at both the senior leader team level and the senior leader duo level.

The analysis of the case study results involved the iterative process of moving between the emergent empirical data and the literature. The limitations of the ambidextrous leadership construct became apparent through this process, so the theoretical emphasis shifted to focusing on paradox as a lens. The case study methodology was therefore deemed appropriate for capturing the longitudinal dimensions and analysing the unique relational elements as shown in Table 1.1.

Table 1.1 Overview of the full research program

Leadership level	Methodology focus	
Senior leadership individuals	Qualitative interviews	*Analysis of qualitative data from general interviews to develop approach to case study*
Senior leadership teams	Qualitative case study	*Case study immersion focusing on the senior leadership team – including 'draw and talk' interview technique and observations*
Senior leadership duos		*Case study immersion focusing on the executive senior leadership duo*

The following chapters explain the process and outcomes of this research program in more detail. Additional quotes from my consulting and research work over the years have also been included here to help illustrate the relevance of the core concepts explored in different contexts.

Notes

1 D'Aveni, 1994, Dess and Picken, 2000, Tushman and O'Reilly, 1996
2 O'Bryan, 2018
3 Mone, McKinley and Barker, 1998
4 Andrew et al., 2010
5 Nyström, 1990
6 Bledow et al., 2009, Smith et al., 2017
7 Smith and Lewis, 2011
8 Jarzabkowski, Lê and Van de Ven, 2013
9 Hargrave and Van de Ven, 2017
10 Smith and Tushman, 2005
11 Amabile, 1996, Miron-Spektor and Erez, 2017
12 Farjoun, 2010
13 Slawinski and Bansal, 2012
14 Siggelkow and Levinthal, 2003
15 Van de Ven et al., 2007
16 Tzeng, 2009
17 Crossan and Apaydin, 2010
18 Crossan and Apaydin, 2010
19 Manz et al., 1989, Mumford et al., 2002, Nemanich and Vera, 2009
20 Eg Eisenbeiss, van Knippenberg and Boerner, 2008, Mumford et al., 2002, Tierney and Farmer, 2002, Zacher and Rosing, 2015
21 Smith and Tushman, 2005
22 Smith and Lewis, 2011
23 Guillemin, 2004
24 Smith, Binns and Tushman, 2010
25 Andriopoulos and Lewis, 2009
26 March, 1991, Tushman and O'Reilley, 1996
27 Smith, 2014

28 Crossland and Hambrick, 2007
29 Schaltegger and Wagner, 2011, p. 223
30 West et al., 2003
31 Mumford and Licuanan, 2004
32 Jansen, Vera and Crossan, 2009, Regnér, 2003
33 Elkins and Keller, 2003, Mumford et al., 2002
34 Lewis and Smith, 2014
35 Smith and Lewis 2011, p. 382
36 Smith and Lewis 2011, p. 396
37 Lewis, 2000
38 Smith, 2014
39 Huff, 1990, Kaplan, 2003, Murnighan and Conlon, 1991
40 Maitlis and Christianson, 2014
41 Balogun and Johnson, 2004
42 Gephart, Topal and Zhang, 2010
43 Donnellon, Gray and Bougon, 1986
44 Jarzabkowski, Lê and Van de Ven, 2013
45 Quinn, Mintzberg and James, 1988
46 Crossan, Lane and White, 1999, Vera and Crossan, 2004
47 Rosing, Frese and Bausch, 2011
48 Maxwell, 2013
49 Becker, 2009
50 Reid and Karambayya, 2016, Rosing, Frese and Bausch, 2011
51 Guest, Bunce and Johnson, 2006

References

Amabile, T. M. (1996). *Creativity and innovation in organizations.* Boston: Harvard Business School.
Andrew, J. P., Manget, J., Michael, D. C., Taylor, A., & Zablit, H. (2010). *Innovation 2010: A return to prominence – and the emergence of a new world order.* Boston: Boston Consulting Group.
Andriopoulos, C., & Lewis, M. W. (2009). Exploitation-exploration tensions and organizational ambidexterity: Managing paradoxes of innovation. *Organization Science, 20*(4), 696–717.
Balogun, J., & Johnson, G. (2004). Organizational restructuring and middle manager sensemaking. *Academy of Management Journal, 47*(4), 523–549.
Becker, H. S. (2009). How to find out how to do qualitative research. *International Journal of Communication, 3*, 545–553.
Bledow, R., Frese, M., Anderson, N., Erez, M., & Farr, J. (2009). A dialectic perspective on innovation: Conflicting demands, multiple pathways, and ambidexterity. *Industrial and Organizational Psychology, 2*(3), 305–337.
Crossan, M. M., & Apaydin, M. (2010). A multi-dimensional framework of organizational innovation: A systematic review of the literature. *Journal of Management Studies, 47*(6), 1154–1191.
Crossan, M. M., Lane, H. W., & White, R. E. (1999). An organizational learning framework: From intuition to institution. *Academy of Management Review, 24*(3), 522–537.
Crossland, C., & Hambrick, D. C. (2007). How national systems differ in their constraints on corporate executives: A study of CEO effects in three countries. *Strategic Management Journal, 28*(8), 767–789.

D'Aveni, R. A. (1994). *Hypercompetition: Managing the dynamics of strategic manoeuvring.* New York: Free Press.

Dess, G. G., & Picken, J. C. (2000). Changing roles: Leadership in the 21st century. *Organizational Dynamics, 28*(3), 18–34.

Donnellon, A., Gray, B., & Bougon, M. G. (1986). Communication, meaning, and organized action. *Administrative Science Quarterly, 31*(1), 43–55.

Eisenbeiss, S. A., van Knippenberg, D., & Boerner, S. (2008). Transformational leadership and team innovation: Integrating team climate principles. *Journal of Applied Psychology, 93*(6), 1438–1446.

Elkins, T., & Keller, R. T. (2003). Leadership in research and development organizations: A literature review and conceptual framework. *Leadership Quarterly, 14*(4–5), 587–606.

Farjoun, M. (2010). Beyond dualism: Stability and change as a duality. *Academy of Management Review, 35*(2), 202–225.

Gephart, R. P., Topal, C., & Zhang, Z. (2010). Future-oriented sensemaking: Temporalities and institutional legitimation. In S. Maitlis & T. Hernes (Eds.), *Process, sensemaking, and organizing* (pp. 275–312). Oxford: Oxford University Press.

Guest, G., Bunce, A., & Johnson, L. (2006). How many interviews are enough? An experiment with data saturation and variability. *Field Methods, 18*(1), 59–82.

Guillemin, M. (2004). Understanding illness: Using drawings as a research method. *Qualitative Health Research, 14*(2), 272–289.

Hargrave, T. J., & Van de Ven, A. H. (2017). Integrating dialectical and paradox perspectives on managing contradictions in organizations. *Organization Studies, 38* (3–4), 319–339.

Huff, A. S. (1990). *Mapping strategic thought.* New York: Harper and Row.

Jansen, J. J., Vera, D., & Crossan, M. (2009). Strategic leadership for exploration and exploitation: The moderating role of environmental dynamism. *The Leadership Quarterly, 20*(1), 5–18.

Jarzabkowski, P., Lê, J. K., & Van de Ven, A. H. (2013). Responding to competing strategic demands: How organizing, belonging, and performing paradoxes coevolve. *Strategic Organization, 11*(3), 245–280.

Kaplan, R. D. (2003). *Warrior politics: Why leadership demands a pagan ethos.* New York: Random House.

Lewis, M. W. (2000). Exploring paradox: Toward a more comprehensive guide. *Academy of Management Review, 25*(4), 760–776.

Lewis, M. W., & Smith, W. K. (2014). Paradox as a metatheoretical perspective: Sharpening the focus and widening the scope. *Journal of Applied Behavioral Science, 50*(2), 127–179.

Maitlis, S., & Christianson, M. (2014). Sensemaking in organizations: Taking stock and moving forward. *Academy of Management Annals, 8*(1), 57–125.

Manz, C. C., Bastien, D. T., Hostager, T. J., & Shapiro, G. L. (1989). Leadership and innovation: A longitudinal process view. In A. H. Van de Ven, H. L. Angle, & M. S. Poole (Eds.), *Research on the management of innovation: The Minnesota studies* (pp. 613–636). Oxford: Oxford University Press.

March, J. G. 1991. Exploration and Exploitation in Organizational Learning. Organization Science, 2(1): 71-87.

Maxwell, J. (2013). *Qualitative research design: An interactive approach.* Thousand Oaks: Sage.

Miron-Spektor, E., & Erez, M. (2017). Looking at creativity through a paradox lens. In W. K. Smith, M. W. Lewis, P. Jarzabkowski, & A. Langley (Eds.), *The Oxford handbook of organizational paradox* (pp. 434–451). New York: Oxford University Press.

Mone, M. A., McKinley, W., & Barker III, V. L. (1998) Organizational decline and innovation: A contingency framework. *Academy of Management Review*, *23*(1), 115–132.

Mumford, M. D., & Licuanan, B. (2004). Leading for innovation: Conclusions, issues, and directions. *Leadership Quarterly*, *15*(1), 163–171.

Mumford, M. D., Scott, G. M., Gaddis, B., & Strange, J. M. (2002). Leading creative people: Orchestrating expertise and relationships, *The Leadership Quarterly*, *13*(6), 705–750.

Murnighan, J. K., & Conlon, D. E. (1991). The dynamics of intense work groups: A study of British string quartets. *Administrative Science Quarterly*, *36*(2), 165–186.

Nemanich, L. A., & Vera, D. (2009). Transformational leadership and ambidexterity in the context of an acquisition. *The Leadership Quarterly*, *20*(1), 19–33.

Nyström, H. (1990). Organizational innovation. In M. A. West & J. L. Farr (Eds.), *Innovation and creativity at work: Psychological and organizational strategies* (pp. 143–161). Oxford: John Wiley and Sons.

O'Bryan, M. (2018). Innovation: The most important and overused word in America. https://www.wired.com/insights/2013/11/innovation-the-most-important-and-overused-word-in-america/

Quinn, J. B., Mintzberg, H., & James, R. M. (1988). *The strategy process: Concepts, contexts, and cases.* Englewood Cliffs: Prentice-Hall.

Regnér, P. (2003). Strategy creation in the periphery: Inductive versus deductive strategy making. *Journal of Management Studies*, *40*(1), 57–82.

Reid, W., & Karambayya, R. (2016). The shadow of history: Situated dynamics of trust in dual executive leadership. *Leadership*, *12*(5), 609–631.

Rosing, K., Frese, M., & Bausch, A. (2011). Explaining the heterogeneity of the leadership-innovation relationship: Ambidextrous leadership. *The Leadership Quarterly*, *22*(5), 956–974.

Schaltegger, S., & Wagner, M. (2011). Sustainable entrepreneurship and sustainability innovation: Categories and interactions. *Business Strategy and the Environment*, *20*(4), 222–237.

Siggelkow, N., & Levinthal, D. A. (2003). Temporarily divide to conquer: Centralized, decentralized, and reintegrated organizational approaches to exploration and adaptation. *Organization Science*, *14*(6), 650–669.

Slawinski, N., & Bansal, P. (2012). A matter of time: The temporal perspectives of organizational responses to climate change. *Organization Studies*, *33*(11), 1537–1563.

Smith, W. K. (2014). Dynamic decision making: A model of senior leaders managing strategic paradoxes. *Academy of Management Journal*, *57*(6), 1592–1623.

Smith, W. K., Binns, A., & Tushman, M. L. (2010). Complex business models: Managing strategic paradoxes simultaneously. *Long Range Planning*, *43*(2), 448–461.

Smith, W. K., Erez, M., Jarvenpaa, S., Lewis, M. W., & Tracey, P. (2017). Adding complexity to theories of paradox, tensions, and dualities of innovation and change: Introduction to organization studies special issue on paradox, tensions, and dualities of innovation and change. *Organization Studies*, *38*(3–4), 303–317.

Smith, W. K., & Lewis, M. W. (2011). Toward a theory of paradox: A dynamic equilibrium model of organizing. *Academy of Management Review*, *36*(2), 381–403.

Smith, W. K., & Tushman, M. L. (2005). Managing strategic contradictions: A top management model for managing innovation streams. *Organization Science, 16*(5), 522–536.

Tierney, P., & Farmer, S. M. (2002). Creative self-efficacy: Its potential antecedents and relationship to creative performance. *Academy of Management Journal, 45*(6), 1137–1148.

Tushman, M. L., & O'Reilly III, C. A. (1996). Ambidextrous organizations: Managing evolutionary and revolutionary change. *California Management Review, 38*(4), 8–29.

Tzeng, C. H. (2009). A review of contemporary innovation literature: A Schumpeterian perspective. *Innovation, 11*(3), 373–394.

Van de Ven, A., Polley, D., Garud, S., & Venkataraman, S. (2007). *The innovation journey*. New York: Oxford University Press.

Vera, D., & Crossan, M. (2004). Strategic leadership and organizational learning. *Academy of Management Review, 29*(2), 222–240.

West, M. A., Borrill, C. S., Dawson, J. F., Brodbeck, F., Shapiro, D. A., & Haward, B. (2003). Leadership clarity and team innovation in health care. *The Leadership Quarterly, 14*(4–5), 393–410.

Zacher, H., & Rosing, K. (2015). Ambidextrous leadership and team innovation. *Leadership & Organization Development Journal, 36*(1), 54–68.

2 Setting the context

Why we need to manage purpose-driven innovation better

OVERVIEW

This chapter explores the *theories* that informed the research approach, and identifies how polarising tensions can easily be generated where there is complexity and rapid change. Through a core case study of a social enterprise rapidly scaling up services to meet client demands a range of core polarising tensions are identified – such as those between purpose and profit, and between breakthrough exploratory innovation and more incremental maintenance functions. How leaders and leadership teams are constantly involved in a 'sensemaking' process as they strategise, make decisions and plan in complex contexts is also discussed. The 'paradox' theoretical lens is outlined as a tool for interpreting how leaders make sense of the polarising tensions in order to navigate them. Rather than pursuing either one polar position or the other, recent paradox research has revealed that it's not only possible

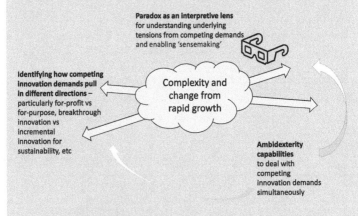

Paradox as an interpretive lens for understanding underlying tensions from competing demands and enabling 'sensemaking'

Identifying how competing innovation demands pull in different directions – particularly for-profit vs for-purpose, breakthrough innovation vs incremental innovation for sustainability, etc

Complexity and change from rapid growth

Ambidexterity capabilities to deal with competing innovation demands simultaneously

Figure 2.1 Understanding the theoretical approach

DOI: 10.4324/9781003426691-2

but also beneficial to pursue both competing simultaneously. Paradox is thus detailed as a useful construct to further understanding how this can be done in practice, and the concept of 'ambidexterity' a model for dealing with competing demands simultaneously is also introduced and explored as a potential management strategy at this level (Figure 2.1).

Making sense of and managing tensions

The day I arrived to start studying the for-purpose organisation I had targeted for this study – Social Support Services (SSO) – a crisis emerged. I soon realised that in fact this was one of many crises that would continue to constantly manifest in quick succession. It was like arriving at an Emergency ward in the hospital.

The immediate crisis was that the government had amended some legislation that would detrimentally impact the organisation's vulnerable clients. There was a great sense of urgency, and it was apparent that the 120+ staff and hundreds of volunteers working in this enterprise were on the coalface, literally helping to save lives. The long-term ongoing crises related to the ever-changing social, economic and government factors which meant the organisation was constantly changing tack to try to keep up.

I had selected to study this organisation as it was known to be particularly innovative, and I knew the work it was doing was of critical importance for their clients. My plan was to conduct some ethnographic research to find out how SSO was able to achieve what it did. My hope was to spend time immersed in the everyday running of the enterprise. I would attend regular meetings, assist with different work tasks to gain an in-depth insight into how things functions and conduct formal and informal interviews at all levels to identify the key stakeholder or influencers and the impact of their actions.

Soon after landing on the doorstep to start the research with SSO, a crisis meeting was called, and I was thrown into the creative chaos of practical innovation in action. The next two years were spent visiting the organisation and being an active 'participant observer', to experience the inner workings at a deeper level rather than simply reporting on what was observable on the surface.

I helped on the reception desk and met the clients facing traumatic experiences and urgently needing medical and legal support. I worked with the Director of the 'Innovation Hub', which was responsible for supporting the longer term education and development programs for the clients. And I sat in on executive meetings to get a feel for how this was all managed. I interviewed a range of people from those with lived experience through to those who had come from corporate backgrounds. It soon became clear to me that, as the new operations leader at the time stated, the organisation was running '... like a bumblebee – it shouldn't fly, but somehow it does'. There was an apparent tension between the need to continue to innovate rapidly to support the fast-changing needs of vulnerable clients, and at the same to ensure stability and structure to build on for sustainable growth.

It's easy to see how rapid change has a significant impact on organisations like this. What can be more difficult to identify is how to effectively deal with the impact. The challenge is that because rapid change will typically generate competing demands, this can lead to significant tension at all levels of an organisation. After spending time working with a number of different types of organisations as both a consultant and a researcher, I was keen to develop a clearer idea of how creative tensions can be harnessed to fuel sustainable innovation. Years of experience with organisations through consulting at the senior leader level, most often in supporting leaders to identify how to create a culture that supports innovation, has led to an interest in investigating innovation leadership in depth. Extensive work with for-purpose organisations with multiple competing demands also exposed the value of effective innovation leadership for fulfilling an organisation's vision and mission.

After all those years of observing these fascinating phenomena, I was looking forward to taking a more rigorous research approach with this case study to get to the core.

How innovation polarities are generated

Factors such as globalisation and rapid technological development have been great disruptors. They have typically led to confronting ambiguities and competing demands. This means that contemporary rapid-change environments are often characterised by complexity and chaos.

This complexity and chaos can then manifest in organisations. As an organisation adopts to these changes, there can be a need for more staff, more income and more support – and then ironically as the diversity and search for resources increases, complexity and chaos become more prevalent.[1] Competing demands such as these are frequently experienced as persistent underlying tensions.[2] The rapid pace of change can also bring these tensions to the surface and demand some sort of resolution.[3] But how do leaders effectively respond to this dilemma?

Although innovation is imperative for survival,[4] a focus on innovation can in itself contribute to the complexity and can produce its own set of competing demands and tensions.[5] Unique tensions related to leadership in organisations seeking to innovate have been identified in the academic literature.[6] Leaders must learn to deal with these multiple competing strategic demands simultaneously.[7] But, it's just not possible to stop everything and deal with a each individual issue in real time.

At the core of these competing demands can be the need both to 'pluralise', or to use future-focused thinking to identify potential alternate realities, and to 'organise', or to work in the present to bring a holistic unity to the organisation.[8] This can be like trying to open and explore a number of different doors positioned over quicksand and explore all possible future options while simultaneously standing your ground and attempting to establish a firm base. It can seem like an impossible task, and at least a deeply destabilising challenge. Yet it is a challenge that must inevitably be faced.

Plurality is both a common feature and a necessary requirement of contemporary organisational life,[9] but it can also lead to a volatile environment.[10] While it is recognised that plurality is related to innovation and growth, organising is also simultaneously required to provide the stability to support that innovation and growth.[11]

Oppositional conditions like these may seem contradictory, yet they can also be understood to be complementary,[12] which can also lead to tensions.[13] The unique competing demands between the need to explore new innovation opportunities while maintaining current systems and structures have been well established for many years now.[14] In the context of innovation, in particular, a significant number of academic studies refer to the need for a focus on breakthrough innovation and growth based on risk taking and pushing the boundaries through *exploration* to meet contemporary demands, acknowledging that this focus can threaten the organisation's stability. Equally important, therefore, is the identified need for incremental innovation through the *exploitation* of current systems and products which can provide a more stable foundation for growth, also acknowledging that an overemphasis on stability as a trade-off can reduce competitiveness and survival in a rapid-change context.[15]

The unique demands of 'for-purpose' innovation

Competing demands can be many and varied. This is particularly the case where an organisation has different strategic goals embedded in its structure.[16]

One of the clearest examples of this is when an organisation is set up for purpose and yet must also be sustainable or profitable.

Think about how tensions from competing demands can proliferate in 'not-for-profit' organisations as an example, since they are often susceptible to rapid change but experience with increasing plurality and resource limitations.[17] Hybrid organisations such as social enterprises in particular are usually required to focus on purpose while also ensuring sustainability and capacity.[18] The importance of ensuring socially responsible and sustainable practices while simultaneously meeting economic imperatives in the innovation context for these organisations has been explored in the literature My exploratory interviews with global innovation leaders helped to cast further light on these unique challenges.[19]

The following quote from an innovation leader of a large not-for-profit organisation describes the tensions from the competing demands:

> The purpose-driven perspective usually (focuses on) satisfying multiple objectives... so that can create quite a lot of competing or misaligned objectives. The other element is: you really are constrained by resources, and that's both in terms of financial as well as people-related resources... So what you have to do is to learn to work with what you've got. The problems are enormous, and therefore trying to identify which are the problems you solve and which that you let go. It can be quite challenging, especially when you got resources, people who joined the organisation with strong passion about particular issues, and that's where you have to interesting and heated debate about what to do and what not to do. So alignment of focus, of direction, choosing what to do and what not to do is probably more pronounced... I suppose the rules are less clear, decision rules.
>
> *Interview with the Head of Innovation of a global*
> *not-for-profit organisation*

The combination of social and business goals in these organisations affects values and identities, and often also results in ethical dilemmas.[20] The polarising effect of dual strategic goals can reinforce paradoxical tensions between business demands and social expectations,[21] as it is often assumed that a focus on purpose in these organisations will require a sacrifice in profit.[22] There can, for example, be tensions in the areas of strategic direction, domain and strategy implementation.[23]

Conversely, as a comparison, leaders of for-profit organisations can experience tensions from competing demands between personal values or aspirational social values and the need to focus on profit.[24]

> She (executive team member) said, 'But be mindful that we're not pursuing a big cause or whatever. We need to make money.' And I said, 'Yea, but, you know, it's shared value, creating shared value,' and she said, 'Oh yea, yea, I know, but no one's interested in that. We're really aiming at selling more.'
>
> *Head of Quality Innovation and Engagement*
> *of a multinational pharmaceutical company*

I also came across similar tensions when I interviewed leaders of for-profit companies seeking to drive sustainable social or environmental change, as demonstrated in the following quote:

> One of the biggest challenges is the complexity of sustainability and sustainable social innovations, because social innovation is only a social innovation, from my point of view, if it's (also) financially sustainable. So you have to develop a model and an approach where you can ensure that, given certain market drivers, solutions can get reach to the market in a sustainable way, which also ensures financial sustainability.
>
> *Interview with Head of Corporate Administration*
> *of a multinational chemical company*

As Smith et al.[25] have explained after studying senior leadership challenges in social enterprises, the results can be powerful when these tensions are addressed:

> Social enterprises can benefit from integrating the competing demands associated with social missions and commercial viability. Pursuing commercial viability promotes efficiency, performance, innovation, and growth. In contrast, social missions elicit passion, motivation, and commitment. Taken together, the dual forces for performance and passion offer a powerful combination that can lead to new solutions to existing challenges.

It is clear that there needs to be more research into *how senior leaders navigate competing demands* such as these, as many leaders are unaware of the underlying tensions and how they influence their actions.[26]

The pressures of scaling-up

Many organisations face challenging dynamics for a range of reasons, but these challenges can become even more complex when an entity expands rapidly and scales up.[27]

Scale-ups are identified as organisations that reach a 20% annual growth in employment or sales turnover for three consecutive years (OECD, 2010) with an initial workforce of more than ten employees at the beginning of this period (OECD, 2007).[28] The case organisation SSO met this criteria and was assessed as being representative of these types of entities, which often struggle with challenges to growth as they constantly expand.[29]

In scale-ups, any pre-existing tensions can be exacerbated, and new organisation and management tensions will often emerge,[30] particularly when there is a transition from the start-up phase to the scale-up phases.[31] These high-growth enterprises will face several unique challenges as they scale up due to unpredictable individuals operating in the potentially volatile complex environmental conditions of rapid change while also dealing with plurality and scarcity of resources.[32] While there is a need to grow operations fast, there is often a lack of resources to enable this,[33] and scale-ups tend to go through a state of constant change as they adapt to shifting environmental contexts.[34] Challenges can include: the challenges of capabilities and systems gaps from increased size,[35] the need for significant resources to cope with the rapid growth and associated resources scarcity,[36] the challenge of incorporating new employees quickly along with the associated culture change issues[37] and higher risk levels such as financial risk.[38]

Adaptation is required, as in the early stages of enterprise development entrepreneur founders need to focus on defining the key opportunity and capitalising on it,[39] such as through product development,[40] but as the organisation grows there needs to be more of a focus on systematisation and strategic planning.[41] Larger more established organisations require more standardised processes, structures and routines to perform at scale.[42]

*How scale-ups experience the tensions between the need
for exploration and exploitation*

The core ambiguity underlining these challenges for scale-ups has been identified as the need to adapt and grow to meet market demands and fulfil the purpose, and a need for stability and efficiency for sustainability.[43]

The conditions of 'growth' and 'stability' can be complementary,[44] as stability is often a precondition for flexibility,[45] while reliability similarly requires adaptation.[46] These conditions are also, however, innately contradictory – which typically leads to a tension between the polar dimensions and necessitates a complex balancing act.[47] This scale-up tension has been found to be best resolved when leaders develop a business model that can help to both create and sustain value.[48]

The tension between these core competing innovation demands, the need for both *exploration* and *exploitation*, is particularly pronounced in rapid growth enterprises – as it is important for the scale-up to focus on both innovation to explore new domains and support growth (exploration) and incremental development to exploit current capabilities for longer term stability (exploitation).[49] This exploration-exploitation tension is often specifically prevalent in scale- ups.[50] Enterprise survival has been found to be linked to pursuing these apparently contradictory goals of change to enact an entrepreneurial opportunity from untapped market potential,[51] along with to develop sustainable support structures to create value.[52]

Paradox as an interpretive lens

Relatively early in my study of this topic, I determined that the concept of 'paradox' could provide a valuable theoretical lens for understanding how leaders make sense of these competing demands.

In the management literature, paradox refers to 'contradictory yet interrelated elements – elements that seem logical in isolation but absurd and irrational when appearing simultaneously',[53] and paradoxes have been defined as leading to tensions that are 'synergistic and persistent'.[54] The basic assumption is that at the heart of these tensions that arise from competing demands are paradoxes which, if not dealt with can frustrate innovation - or if identified and managed effectively, can support or even fuel sustainable innovation and growth.[55]

Think about how rocket fuel is both highly flammable and dangerous, yet it can take a rocket to the moon and back. If not handled correctly, tensions can also be destructive and divisive, leading to conflict and stymieing the best of plans. Yet when handled well, the potent power can provide a great boost to support constructive creative change. I found this paradox framework can help to identify the impact of underlying tensions from a range of competing demands that emerge as organisations innovate and grow, and to explain how these tensions can manifest and be addressed.[56]

The paradoxes that arise in complex innovation contexts are not merely dualisms or dilemmas that can be readily 'solved' through simple separation strategies. Studies have identified that there is a need to pursue competing paradoxical demands interdependently rather than choosing between them as dualities,[57] which can exacerbate the challenges.

Consider some of the competing demands and associated tensions that might be identified in leading in innovation contexts and how both poles of the paradox need to be addressed equally. These polar tensions might include the need to: explore breakthrough new innovation opportunities while maintaining current systems and structures,[58] generate new ideas and also implement ideas,[59] allow for diversity and adaptability along with ensuring consistency,[60] plan for the future while focusing on survival in the present[61] and enable centralisation along with allowing for decentralisation.[62] Additional tensions in these contexts might include: generating new ideas versus ensuring innovation implementation,[63] idealism versus pragmatism,[64] mechanistic versus organic structures,[65] global versus local needs,[66] new and old,[67] autocracy versus democracy,[68] individual versus collective demands[69] and local search versus 'long jump'.[70]

In complex contexts, competing demands are not experienced in isolation and can emerge at any point in time.[71] Multiple demands can come from any level: from the societal context, from organisational structures and expectations and from individual differences such as values, assumptions and practices.[72] So these multiple demands can then also lead to tensions between sub-groups with divergent values.[73]

A model for dealing with competing innovation demands

It's easy to think and act in black and white. Where there are competing demands, we will most likely see it as a trade-off. We think we will need to focus on one *OR* the other.

According to the latest theories, though, addressing paradox effectively requires a 'both/and' strategy rather than an 'either/or' approach.[74] This involves pursuing both goals simultaneously to reach a more fluid position of 'dynamic equilibrium'.[75] Although it was once believed that the impact of paradoxical tensions should be minimised,[76] there is an increasing awareness of the importance of recognising and accepting these tensions. Pursuing paradoxical goals simultaneously is now seen as the essential course of action for the organisation to remain competitive and viable.[77]

Managing paradoxical tensions involves[78] *identifying the tensions* that create polarisation (cognitive or social constructions), *recognising potential vicious cycles* that could be reinforcing the tensions and *structuring synthesising solutions* that might help to deal with the tensions created by the paradoxes more effectively. In this context, a transcendent approach is recommended, which includes the initial steps of accepting and confronting these tensions rather than avoiding them or compromising.[79] By helping to identify the underlying tensions and address them,[80] leaders will be better equipped to deal with competing demands.[81]

Once the tensions are acknowledged (identifying opposition), it is important to address the two poles of the tension at two different locations (spatial separation) or points in time (temporal separation), and then to introduce a new element that will accommodate both (synthesis).[82] This could mean, for example, discussing the different competing demands, then talking through what roles or in what parts of the organisation or in what processes each polar position can be addressed (spatial separation). There could be some roles and/ or departments (like typically R&D) that focus on 'exploration', while others (such as finance) focus on 'exploitation'. Other potential solutions could involve identifying at what stages of a process the different needs could be addressed (temporal separation) – such as at the beginning of a project there could be a focus on the 'exploration' of breakthrough new ideas through a brainstorming phase, and further into the process there could be a focus on 'exploitation' through the testing, prototyping and incremental development of ideas to prepare for implementation.

These management strategies involve learning to live with rather than trying to resolve the tensions[83] – since the tensions can and should, in fact, be productive to help fuel innovation. They enable leaders to deal with polar positions simultaneously while addressing the potential for inertia if both of these poles are not addressed.[84]

This approach to simultaneous management is often referred to in the literature as 'organisation ambidexterity'.[85] It has been suggested that developing ambidexterity, or balancing paradoxical competing yet complementary tensions through a paradox framework, will assist with the development of innovative capabilities[86] and innovative performance.[87] Ambidexterity is understood to support both adaptation and maintenance functions and assist with effective change management.[88] Identifying and managing paradoxical tensions in innovation contexts has been found to facilitate ambidexterity.[89]

The literature on organisation ambidexterity is extensive[90] and covers a range of different areas such as organisation economics,[91] organisational theory,[92] new product development[93] and technological innovation.[94] Literature streams that have contributed to the evolution of the concept of organisational ambidexterity include: organisational learning, technological innovation, organisational adaptation, strategic management and organisational design.

Although previous recommendations for addressing the ambiguities and associated tensions have included externalising exploitation or exploration activities – for example, through outsourcing or partnership alliances[95] or temporary cycling between periods of exploration and exploitation[96] – these approaches do not involve simultaneous focus and therefore do not appropriately meet the requirements for organisation ambidexterity.[97]

Scholars have used the notion of ambidexterity to explain how established companies manage explore-exploit tensions by pursuing exploration and exploitation at the same time. The established applications include structural and contextual ambidexterity.[98] Structural ambidexterity refers to building ambidextrous functions into the organisation strategies and systems also that they can operate simultaneously. This might include, as an example, operating an exploration business unit in parallel with exploiting a more established business unit. Contextual ambidexterity refers to the practice of embedding ambidextrous principles and practices into behavioural functions at the individual and unit level so that all members of the organisation become responsible for implementing ambidexterity in their daily work.

Actions required to facilitate organisational ambidexterity include[99]:

1 **Initiation:** developing a strategic approach once the tensions have been identified
2 **Contextualisation:** putting organisation systems and structures in place to address the paradox
3 **Implementation**: managing the paradoxes in everyday practices

Empirical evidence has demonstrated there is a positive interaction effect between exploitation and exploration learning at the organisation level which can lead to longer term sustainability,[100] and a relationship between organisational ambidexterity and performance at the business unit level has been identified.[101]

Organisation structures, behavioural contexts and leadership processes have all been recognised as important factors that impact organisation ambidexterity.[102] However, fewer studies have focused on individual ambidexterity[103] and ambidextrous leadership,[104] which are relatively newer constructs in the literature.[105] As in organisation ambidexterity, the literature on individual ambidexterity has also established that ambidexterity requires both exploration and exploitation.[106] Recent literature has identified that individual ambidexterity is also an important antecedent for innovative problem-solving and effective innovation management.[107]

Making sense of sensemaking

So what is the best way to understand and interpret complex phenomena such as these? The best approach is recognised as gaining an authentic insight into how leaders think and act. This involves identifying and analysing how leaders *make sense of* the tensions and manage them as they experience them and following key incidents and events – which is known as 'sensemaking'.

Leaders typically make sense of organisational tensions and related ambiguities through this sensemaking process, which is known to involve both cognitive and discursive framing.[108] That means that uncovering both mental processes and conversational cues can help to reveal the underlying processes at work. I therefore adopted a sensemaking perspective to explore how senior leaders and leadership teams experience and manage competing paradoxical demands, and how they 'interpret' these tensions individually and collectively and 'integrate' for collective action.[109]

Sensemaking is recognised as a means of dealing with complexity and uncertainty, particularly where there is ambiguity.[110] When engaged in sensemaking, individuals and groups interpret and reflect on phenomena as a form of meaning processing.[111] As it provides a window into a deeper world, understanding sensemaking in practice has become a widely used framework for identifying and understanding how individuals and groups respond to organisational challenges.[112] The sensemaking approach identifies both critical and creative thinking as a means of making 'sense' of challenging situations and provides a useful framework for understanding how tensions are managed,[113] particularly in the innovation context.

Sensemaking has been described as 'a kind of creative authoring' and a form of framing and filtering that is 'a search for plausibility and coherence, that is reasonable and memorable, which embodies past experience and expectations, and maintains the self while resonating with others... (and which) can be constructed retrospectively yet used prospectively, and captures thoughts and emotions.'[114]

Often labels and categories are applied in the sensemaking process to provide some consistency and coherence and facilitate concrete actions,[115] particularly in the group context.[116] When these labels are used, sensemaking processes can enable simultaneous interpretation and action.[117] Sensemaking therefore also provides a useful means for exploring the underlying group dynamics that can lead to team consensus.[118] It works from the premise that individuals construct their version of reality using available cognitive frames as a means of shaping perceptions and actions.[119] Often these frames are shared and negotiated through discursive practices in order to create a form of social scaffolding.

While there has been extensive exploration in the literature of the individual sensemaking process in dealing with competing demands,[120] there has been less of an emphasis on collective sensemaking processes within teams.[121] Additionally, the literature on group responses has focused on collective responses to emergencies and crisis situations, and the findings do not always apply in a range of organisation contexts.[122] For example, the literature is not clear on how individual views and differences are negotiated to produce a collective consensus on how to make sense of and respond to tensions, even though this is a common practice for senior leadership teams.

The creative act of collective sensemaking

It's challenging enough to understand individual sensemaking practices. But add the complex dynamics of a group and the task is especially difficult. Individuals have very different ways of understanding reality that cannot always be resolved through calculated or logical reasoning and negotiation.[123] Individual sensemaking has also been found to be related to preferred identity narratives, so unraveling these in a social context is tricky.[124]

It's worth making the effort, though, as it has been found that the opportunity to develop innovative problem-solving approaches can be enhanced in the collective sensemaking context. Creative thinking 'is fueled through the new belief structures that emerge from multi-party sensemaking'.[125]

Yet a number of tensions are inherent in the process of collective sensemaking. While sensemaking requires coherence,[126] differentiation in relation to task, experience and context can hinder attempts at group cohesion.

Collective sensemaking in rapid-change contexts involves unstructured connections between individuals,[127] and cause-and-effect relationships often develop as part of the sensemaking process,[128] so narratives that weave these elements together can readily become a means of collective sensemaking.[129] Shared interpretations of events can evolve into stories of specific genres and types.[130] These stories can then become meaningfully embedded in or integrated into the institutional framework of an organisation.[131] Shared stories can eventually develop into a means of coherence, not only enabling logical consistency but also coalescing the various individual strands and disparate frames.

This is why there is often so much of an emphasis now on clarifying the vision, mission and values in an organisation – in order to create a narrative that will consolidate the diverse elements and provide important scaffolding to build on. The official and unofficial stories can become 'temporal, discursive constructions that provide a means for individual, social and organizational sensemaking and sensegiving'.[132] Jointly negotiated stories, such as vision and mission statements that have been produced in a collaborative workshop, simultaneously support collective sensemaking[133] and represent the process.[134] These mutually reinforcing stories then facilitate strategic action, as 'without requisite consonance between actors' narrativized understandings the interlocking routines and habituated action patterns that serve as centripetal forces binding people together around the same activities, and in the same time and place, will dissolve'.[135]

However, the link between sensemaking and story is yet to be studied in detail,[136] particularly in relation to collective sensemaking.

Can sensemaking be coordinated?

A number of studies have demonstrated that it is possible to achieve shared sensemaking even where there are diverging orientations,[137] but how this happens is not yet clear.

According to one theoretical stream, collective sensemaking is implicit in organisation socialisation[138] through the development of a shared frame of reference,[139] which enables the 'bracketing' or linking of situational cues to facilitate coordinated action.[140] This means that as individuals naturally socialise, they inevitably find ways to connect to enable collaborative action.

According to another theoretical stream, collective sensemaking requires deliberate coordinated reflection and action. The theorists in this stream assert that the combination of individual frames of reference leads to different sensemaking orientations and tensions, despite the presence of concurrent collaborative actions.[141] Individuals in groups, they say, need to negotiate a 'truce' to deal with competitive approaches to framing,[142] such as through referring to boundary objects that help provide definition.[143] Think of how specific policies, guidelines or rules might serve this purpose of assisting with coordinating action.

There is still, however, a lack of clarity around how teams collectively categorise events and build schemas that can lead to productive collective action.[144] Previous research into this demonstrates how the sensemaking process can progress from the individual level to the collective level through.[145]

1 **Intuiting**: individual sensemaking
2 **Interpreting**: sharing at the group level
3 **Integrating**: agreeing on as a collective understanding
4 **Institutionalising**: determining appropriate organisation applications

Some theorists have focused on organisational action as the clear product of consensus in sensemaking, but this approach often fails to acknowledge the role of discrepant sensemaking between individuals.[146] Others have recognised that some shared understanding is required for organised action without focusing on how this happens.[147]

The specific dynamics that contribute to the schema building involved in sensemaking and meaning construction need to be studied in greater detail to understand how this process works.

The importance of leadership sensemaking

If you're trying to understand leadership cognition and action, as I was in this study, you'll need to consider the collective sensemaking practices of the senior leadership team. Leadership teams are the engine room of the organisation.

The strategic work of senior leadership teams is particularly contingent on collective sensemaking.[148] Strategising involves an amalgamation of goal-directed activities that will impact the effectiveness and survival of the organisation.[149] The interpretation of events senior leadership team members face will therefore deeply influence this strategy work.[150] The senior leadership team will be constantly involved in the social process of meaning construction for themselves and others as they make sense of the complex changes organisations constantly encounter in the course of strategic planning and action.[151] In order for coordinated strategising and organisation action to occur, 'equivalent understandings' need to be adopted and 'consonance' needs to be reached through mutually reinforcing sensemaking stories.[152]

Where there are competing demands deriving from divergent ideals and realities, such as in not-for-profits and social enterprises, understanding how collective sensemaking occurs and how sensemaking stories and practice converge into strategic action will provide particularly valuable insights into how senior leadership teams function.[153]

A more detailed understanding of how consensus is reached through collective sensemaking in the context not-for-profit organisations or social enterprises is therefore imperative.[154]

REFLECTION AND ACTION QUESTIONS

Reflection

- How common do you think these 'exploration' and 'exploitation' innovation tensions are? Do you think they are relevant for contemporary workplace contexts? Why or why not?
- What extra dimension or level of pressure do you think for-purpose organisations experience? Why?
- What is the value of ambidexterity?
- How do you think learning to identify sensemaking processes can help to uncover underlying motivations and dynamics?

Action

- Can you identify a study or work scenario that would be an interesting purpose-driven innovation case to study?
  - Why would this story be relevant for this context?
  - Who are the key actors and what are the key roles involved?
  - What were the areas of tensions experienced?
  - What makes the story interesting – what were the key challenges and opportunities?

- Describe or draw the initial sensemaking process from the case you have identified, including:
  - Interactions
  - Key conversations

- Try applying the paradox theoretical lens to assist with understanding how the tensions in this case were experienced and addressed.

Notes

1 Grobman, 2005
2 Patriotta and Brown, 2011
3 Farjoun, 2010, Poole and Van de Ven, 2004
4 Finkelstein and Hambrick, 1996

5 Smith and Lewis, 2011
6 Andriopoulos and Lewis, 2009
7 Smith, Binns and Tushman, 2010
8 Glynn, Barr and Dacin, 2000
9 Cyert and March, 1963, Glynn, Barr and Dacin, 2000, Lewis, 2000, Nord, 1978, Thompson, 1967
10 Eisenhardt, 2000
11 Leana and Barry, 2000
12 Bateson, 1972, Weick and Roberts, 1993
13 Farjoun, 2010
14 Andriopoulos and Lewis, 2009, Jay, 2013, Lewis et al., 2002, March 1991, Miron-Spektor, Erez and Naveh, 2004, Smith and Tushman, 2005, Tushman and O'Reilly, 1996
15 March 1991, Andriopoulos and Lewis, 2009, Tushman and O'Reilly, 1996
16 Jay, 2013
17 Smith and Lewis, 2011
18 Besharov and Smith, 2014, Bowman, 2011, Dacin, Dacin and Tracey, 2011; Smith, Besharov, Wessels and Chertok, 2012
19 Schaltegger and Wagner, 2011
20 Smith, Gonin and Besharov, 2013
21 Lewis, 2000, Smith and Lewis, 2011
22 Smith et al., 2012
23 Van der Byl and Slawinski, 2015
24 Parrish, 2010
25 Smith et al. (2012, p. 466)
26 Smith, 2014
27 Es-Sajjade et al., 2021, Grobman, 2005, Shepherd and Patzelt, 2021, 2022
28 Dumont and Zurn, 2007
29 Lee, 2014
30 Demir et al., 2017, Coad, 2009.
31 Churchill and Lewis, 2002, Hmieleski and Ensley, 2007, Mueller et al., 2012
32 Grobman, 2005
33 Ambos et al., 2008, Kor et al., 2007
34 Ensley et al., 2006
35 Busenitz, 1999
36 Ensley et al., 2003
37 Nicholls-Nixon, 2005
38 Dollinger, 1999
39 Carter et al., 1996
40 Hambrick and Crozier, 1985
41 Hanks and Chandler, 1994
42 Mom et al., 2007
43 Levie and Lichtenstein, 2010
44 Leana and Barry, 2000
45 Bateson, 2000
46 Weick and Roberts, 1993
47 Farjoun, 2010
48 Levie and Lichtenstein, 2010
49 Levie and Lichtenstein, 2010
50 Levie and Lichetenstein, 2010, Sarasvathy, 2001
51 Adler and Obstfeld, 2007
52 Lichtenstein et al., 2007
53 Lewis, 2000, p. 760
54 Smith and Lewis, 2011, p. 396

55   Lewis, 2000
56   Lewis and Smith, 2014
57   Smith and Lewis, 2011
58   Smith and Tushman, 2005
59   Amabile, 1996, Miron-Spektor and Erez, 2017
60   Farjoun, 2010
61   Slawinski and Bansal, 2012
62   Siggelkow and Levinthal, 2003
63   Amabile, 1996, Makri and Scandura, 2010, Miron-Spektor and Erez, 2017
64   Ashforth and Reingen, 2014
65   Burns and Stalker, 1961
66   Marquis and Battilana, 2009
67   Dougherty, 1996
68   Quinn, 1984
69   Murnighan and Conlon, 1991
70   Levinthal, 1997
71   Sheep, Fairhurst and Khazanchi, 2017
72   Thornton, Ocasio and Lounsbury, 2012
73   Pratt and Rafaeli, 1997
74   Smith, Binns and Tushman, 2010
75   Smith and Lewis, 2011
76   as explained by Schad et al., 2016
77   Lewis, 2000, Papachroni, Heracleous and Paroutis, 2015, Smith and Lewis, 2011
78   Lewis, 2000
79   Lüscher and Lewis, 2008
80   Smith and Lewis, 2011
81   Knight and Paroutis, 2017, Miron-Spektor, Erez and Naveh, 2011
82   Hahn et al., 2010, Poole and Van de Ven, 1989
83   Poole and Van de Ven, 2010
84   Scherer, Palazzo, and Seidl, 2013, Smith and Tushman, 2005
85   Lin and McDonough, 2011
86   Lin and McDonough 2011
87   Rosing and Zacher, 2017
88   Abdallah, Denis, and Langley, 2011
89   Cameron and Quinn, 1988, Gibson and Birkinshaw, 2004, Poole and Van de Ven, 1989, Smith and Tushman, 2005
90   Benner and Tushman, 2003, Gibson and Birkinshaw, 2004, Raisch and Birkinshaw, 2008
91   Ghemawat and Ricart Costa, 1993
92   Van den Bosch, Volberda and De Boer, 1999
93   Katila and Ahuja, 2002
94   He and Wong, 2004
95   Holmqvist, 2004, Lavie and Rosenkopf, 2006
96   Siggelkow and Levinthal, 2003, Venkatraman, Lee and Iyer, 2007
97   March 1991
98   Tushman and O'Reilly, 1996
99   Raisch and Zimmerman, 2017
100 He and Wong, 2004
101 Gibson and Birkinshaw, 2004
102 Raisch and Birkinshaw, 2008
103 Bledow et al., 2009, Nemanich and Vera, 2009
104 Rosing, Frese and Bausch, 2011
105 Mu et al., 2022, Snehvrat et al., 2018-
106 Chang et al., 2024, Miron-Spektor, Erez, and Naveh, 2004, Mom et al., 2019

107 Miron-Spektor, Erez, and Naveh, 2004, Rosing and Zacher, 2017.
108 Weick, 1995
109 Crossan, Lane and White, 1999, Mintzberg, Ahlstrand and Lampel, 2001, Vera and Crossan, 2004
110 Merkus et al., 2017
111 Bean and Hamilton, 2006, Leiter, 1980, Stein, 2004
112 Weick, Sutcliffe and Obstfeld, 2005
113 Weick, 2009
114 Brown, Stacey and Nandhakumar, 2008, p. 1038
115 Patriotta and Brown, 2011
116 Brown, Colville and Pye, 2015, Höllerer, Jancsary and Grafström, 2018
117 Weick, Sutcliffe and Obstfeld, 2005
118 Cornelissen, Mantere and Vaara, 2014
119 Cornelissen, Mantere and Vaara 2014
120 Hill and Levenhagen, 1995
121 Adner and Helfat, 2003, Finkelstein and Hambrick, 1996
122 Cornelissen, Mantere and Vaara 2014
123 Berger and Luckmann, 1966
124 Brown, Stacey and Nandhakumar, 2008
125 Maitlis and Christianson, 2014, p. 92
126 Weick, 1995
127 Ocasio, Loewenstein and Nigam, 2015
128 Strang and Meyer, 1993
129 Vaara and Tienari, 2011
130 Boje and Rosile, 2003
131 Höllerer, Jancsary and Grafström, 2018
132 Vaara, Sonenshein and Boje, 2016, p. 496
133 Currie and Brown, 2003
134 Berry, 2001
135 Brown, Stacey and Nandhakumar, 2008, p. 1056
136 Brown, Stacey and Nandhakumar, 2008
137 Bergeron and Cooren, 2012; Morgeson, DeRue and Karam, 2009; Patriotta, 2003a; Silva et al., 2014; Vlaar, Van Fenema and Tiwari, 2008
138 eg Harris, 1994; Kaplan, 2008
139 Arnaud and Mills, 2012; Vlaar, Van den Bosch and Volberda, 2006; Vlaar, Van Fenema and Tiwari, 2008
140 Merkus et al., 2017
141 Das and Teng, 2000
142 Merkus, De Heer and Veenswijk, 2014
143 Wolbers and Boersma, 2013
144 Holt and Cornelissen, 2014, Maitlis and Christianson, 2014, Maitlis and Sonenshein, 2010, Sandberg and Tsoukas, 2015, Weick, Sutcliffe and Obstfeld, 2005
145 Crossan, Lane and White, 1999, Mintzberg, Ahlstrand and Lampel, 2001, Vera and Crossan, 2004
146 Louis, 1983, Pfeffer, 1981
147 Donnellon, Gray and Bougon, 1986, Weick, 1979
148 Garreau, Mouricou and Grimand, 2015, Gioia and Chittipeddi, 1991, Maitlis and Lawrence, 2007
149 Jarzabkowski, 2005
150 Balogun and Johnson, 2004, Rouleau and Balogun, 2011, Stigliani and Ravasi, 2012
151 Balogun et al., 2014
152 Brown, Stacey and Nandhakumar, 2008, p. 1056
153 Leiserowitz, Kates and Parris, 2006, Muñoz and Cohen, 2018
154 Boltanski and Thevenot, 2006

34 *Setting the context*

References

Abdallah, C., Denis, J. L., & Langley, A. (2011). Having your cake and eating it too: Discourses of transcendence and their role in organizational change dynamics. *Journal of Organizational Change Management, 24*(3), 333–348.

Adler, P. S., & Obstfeld, D. (2007). The role of affect in creative projects and exploratory search. *Industrial and Corporate Change, 16*(1), 19–50.

Adner, R., & Helfat, C. (2003). Corporate effects and dynamic managerial capabilities. *Strategic Management Journal, 24*(10), 1011–1025.

Amabile, T. M. (1996). Creativity and innovation in organizations. Boston: Harvard Business School.

Ambos, T. C., Mäkelä, K., Birkinshaw, J., & d'Este, P. (2008). When does university research get commercialized? Creating ambidexterity in research institutions. *Journal of Management Studies, 45*(8), 1424–1447.

Andriopoulos, C., & Lewis, M. W. (2009). Exploitation-exploration tensions and organizational ambidexterity: Managing paradoxes of innovation. *Organization Science, 20*(4), 696–717.

Arnaud, N., & Mills, C. E. (2012). Understanding interorganizational agency: A communication perspective. *Group & Organization Management, 37*(4), 452–485.

Ashforth, B. E., & Reingen, P. H. (2014). Functions of dysfunction: Managing the dynamics of an organizational duality in a natural food cooperative. *Administrative Science Quarterly, 53*(3), 474–516.

Balogun, J., Jacobs, C., Jarzabkowski, P., Mantere, S., & Vaara, E. (2014). Placing strategy discourse in context: Sociomateriality, sensemaking, and power. *Journal of Management Studies, 51*(2), 175–201.

Balogun, J., & Johnson, G. (2004). Organizational restructuring and middle manager sensemaking. *Academy of Management Journal, 47*(4), 523–549.

Bateson, G. (1972). *Steps to an ecology of mind: Collected essays in anthropology, psychiatry, evolution, and epistemology.* Chicago: University of Chicago Press.

Bateson, G. (2000). *Steps to an ecology of mind: Collected essays in anthropology, psychiatry, evolution, and epistemology.* Chicago, IL: University of Chicago Press.

Bean, C. J., & Hamilton, F. E. (2006). Leader framing and follower sensemaking: Response to downsizing in the brave new workplace. *Human Relations, 53*(3), 321–349.

Benner, M., & Tushman. M. (2003). Process management and technological innovation: A longitudinal study of the photography and paint industry. *Administrative Science Quarterly, 47*(4), 676–706.

Berger, P. L., & Luckmann, T. (1966). *The social construction of reality.* New York: Anchor.

Bergeron, C. D., & Cooren, F. (2012). The collective framing of crisis management: A ventriloqual analysis of emergency operations centres. *Journal of Contingencies and Crisis Management, 20*(3), 120–137.

Berry, G. R. (2001). Telling stories: Making sense of the environmental behavior of chemical firms. *Journal of Management Inquiry, 10*(1), 58–73.

Besharov, M. L., & Smith, W. K. (2014). Multiple institutional logics in organizations: Explaining their varied nature and implications. *Academy of Management Review, 39*(3), 364–381.

Bledow, R., Frese, M., Anderson, N., Erez, M., & Farr, J. (2009). A dialectic perspective on innovation: Conflicting demands, multiple pathways, and ambidexterity. *Industrial and Organizational Psychology*, *2*(3), 305–337.

Boje, D. M., & Rosile, G. A. (2003). Life imitates art: Enron's epic and tragic narration. *Management Communication Quarterly*, *17*(1), 85–125.

Boltanski, L., & Thévenot, L. (2006). *On justification: Economies of worth* (vol. 27). Princeton: Princeton University Press.

Bowman, W. (2011). Financial capacity and sustainability of ordinary nonprofits. *Nonprofit Management and Leadership*, *22*(1), 37–51.

Brown, A. D., Colville, I., & Pye, A. (2015). Making sense of sensemaking in organization studies. *Organization Studies*, *36*(2), 265–277.

Brown, A. D., Stacey, P., & Nandhakumar, J. (2008). Making sense of sensemaking narratives. *Human Relations*, *61*(8), 1035–1062.

Burns, T., & Stalker, G. M. (1961). *The management of innovation*. London: Tavistock.

Busenitz, L. W. (1999). Entrepreneurial risk and strategic decision making: It'sa matter of perspective. *The Journal of Applied Behavioral Science*, *35*(3), 325–340.

Cameron, K., & Quinn, R. E. (1988). Organizational paradox and transformation. In R. E. S. Quinn, & K. S. Cameron (Eds.), *Paradox and transformation: Toward a theory of change in organization and management, Ballinger series on innovation and organizational change* (pp. 1–18). Cambridge: Ballinger.

Carter, N. M., Gartner, W. B., & Reynolds, P. D. (1996). Exploring start-up event sequences. *Journal of Business Venturing*, *11*(3), 151–166.

Chang, Y. Y., Chapman, G., Hughes, P., & Chang, C. Y. (2024). Individual ambidexterity, relational context and academic entrepreneurship performance: Too much of a good thing? *British Journal of Management*, *35*(2), p.750–774.

Churchill, N. C., & Lewis, V. L. (2002). The five stages of small business growth. *Entrepreneurship: Critical Perspectives on Business and Management*, *3*, 83.

Coad, A. (2009). *The growth of firms: A survey of theories and empirical evidence*. Cheltenham: Edward Elgar Publishing.

Cornelissen, J. P., Mantere, S., & Vaara, E. (2014). The contraction of meaning: The combined effect of communication, emotions, and materiality on sensemaking in the Stockwell shooting. *Journal of Management Studies*, *51*(5), 699–735.

Crossan, M. M., Lane, H. W., & White, R. E. (1999). An organizational learning framework: From intuition to institution. *Academy of Management Review*, *24*(3), 522–537.

Currie, G., & Brown, A. D. (2003). A narratological approach to understanding processes of organizing in a UK hospital. *Human Relations*, *56*(5), 563–586.

Cyert, R. M., & March, J. G. (1963) *A behavioral theory of the firm*. New York: McGraw-Hill.

Dacin, M. T., Dacin, P. A., & Tracey, P. (2011). Social entrepreneurship: A critique and future directions. *Organization Science*, *22*(5), 1203–1213.

Das, T. K., & Teng, B. S. (2000). Instabilities of strategic alliances: An internal tensions perspective. *Organization Science*, *11*(1), 77–101.

Demir, R., Wennberg, K., & McKelvie, A. (2017). The strategic management of high-growth firms: A review and theoretical conceptualization. *Long Range Planning*, *50*(4), 431–456.

Dollinger, M. J. (1999). *Entrepreneurship: Strategies and resources* (2nd ed.). Upper Saddle River: Prentice Hall.

Donnellon, A., Gray, B., & Bougon, M. G. (1986). Communication, meaning, and organized action. *Administrative Science Quarterly, 31*(1), 43–55.

Dougherty, D. (1996). Organizing for innovation. In S. R. Clegg, C. Hardy, & W. R. Nord (Eds.), *Handbook of organization studies*. Thousand Oaks: Sage.

Dumont, J. C., & Zurn, P. (2007). *International migration of health professionals: New evidence and recent trends*. Geneva: A Call to Action: Ensuring Global Human Resources for Health.

Duncan, R. B. (1976). The ambidextrous organization: Designing dual structures for innovation. In R. H. Kilmann, L. R. Pondy, & D. Slevin (Eds.), *The management of organization* (pp. 167–188). New York: North-Holland.

Eisenhardt, K. M. (2000). Paradox, spirals, ambivalence: The new language of change and pluralism. *Academy of Management Review, 25*(4), 703–705.

Ensley, M. D., Hmieleski, K. M., & Pearce, C. L. (2006). The importance of vertical and shared leadership within new venture top management teams: Implications for the performance of startups. *The Leadership Quarterly, 17*(3), 217–231.

Ensley, M. D., Pearson, A., & Pearce, C. L. (2003). Top management team process, shared leadership, and new venture performance: A theoretical model and research agenda. *Human Resource Management Review, 13*(2), 329–346.

Es-Sajjade, A., Pandza, K., & Volberda, H. (2021). Growing pains: Paradoxical tensions and vicious cycles in new venture growth. *Strategic Organization, 19*(1), 37–69.

Farjoun, M. (2010). Beyond dualism: Stability and change as a duality. Academy of Management Review, 35(2), 202–225.

Finkelstein, S., & Hambrick, D. C. (1996). *Strategic leadership: Top executives and their effects on organizations*. Minneapolis: West Publishing Company.

Garreau, L., Mouricou, P., & Grimand, A. (2015). Drawing on the map: An exploration of strategic sensemaking /giving practices using visual representations. *British Journal of Management, 26*(4), 689–712.

Ghemawat, P., & Ricart Costa, J. E. I. (1993). The organizational tension between static and dynamic efficiency. *Strategic Management Journal, 14*(2), 59–73.

Gibson, C. B., & Birkinshaw, J. (2004). The antecedents, consequences, and mediating role of organizational ambidexterity. *The Academy of Management Journal, 47*(2), 209–226.

Gioia, D., & Chittipeddi, K. (1991). Sensemaking and sensegiving in strategic change initiation. *Strategic Management Journal, 12*(6), 433–448.

Glynn, M. A., Barr, P. S., & Dacin, M. T. (2000). Pluralism and the problem of variety. *Academy of Management Review, 25*(4), 726–734.

Grobman, G. M. (2005). Complexity theory: A new way to look at organizational change. *Public Administration Quarterly, 29*(3), 350–382.

Hahn, T., Figge, F., Pinkse, J., & Preuss, L. (2010).Trade-offs in corporate sustainability: You can't have your cake and eat it. *Business Strategy and the Environment, 19*(4), 217–229.

Hambrick, D. C., & Crozier, L. M. (1985). Stumblers and stars in the management of rapid growth. *Journal of Business Venturing, 1*(1), 31–45.

Hanks, S. H., & Chandler, G. N. (1994). Patterns of functional specialization in emerging high tech. *Journal of Small Business Management, 32*(2), 23.

Harris, S. G. (1994). Organizational culture and individual sensemaking: A schema-based perspective. *Organization Science, 5*(3), 309–321.

He, Z. L., & Wong, P. K. (2004). Exploration vs. exploitation: An empirical test of the ambidexterity hypothesis. *Organization Science, 15*(4), 481–494.

Hill, R. C., & Levenhagen, M. (1995). Metaphors and mental models: Sensemaking and sensegiving in innovative and entrepreneurial activities. *Journal of Management, 21*(6), 1057–1074.

Hmieleski, K. M., & Ensley, M. D. (2007). A contextual examination of new venture performance: Entrepreneur leadership behavior, top management team heterogeneity, and environmental dynamism. *Journal of Organizational Behavior: The International Journal of Industrial, Occupational and Organizational Psychology and Behavior, 28*(7), 865–889.

Höllerer, M. A., Jancsary, D., & Grafström, M. (2018). A picture is worth a thousand words: Multimodal sensemaking of the global financial crisis. *Organization Studies, 39*(5–6), 617–644.

Holmqvist, M. (2004). Experiential learning processes of exploitation and exploration within and between organizations: An empirical study of product development. *Organization Science, 15*(1), 70–81.

Holt, R., & Cornelissen, J. (2014). Sensemaking revisited. *Management Learning, 45*(5), 525–539.

Jansen, J. J., Vera, D., & Crossan, M. (2009). Strategic leadership for exploration and exploitation: The moderating role of environmental dynamism. *The Leadership Quarterly, 20*(1), 5–18.

Jarzabkowski, P. (2005). *Strategy as practice: An activity based approach.* New York: Sage.

Jay, J. (2013). Navigating paradox as a mechanism of change and innovation in hybrid organizations. *Academy of Management Journal, 56*(1), 137–159.

Kaplan, S. (2008). Framing contests: Strategy making under uncertainty. *Organization Science, 19*(5), 729–752.

Katila, R., & Ahuja, G. (2002). Something old, something new: A longitudinal study of search behavior and new product introduction. *Academy of Management Journal, 45*(6), 1183–1194.

Knight, E., & Paroutis, S. (2017). Becoming salient: The TMT leader's role in shaping the interpretive context of paradoxical tensions. *Organization Studies, 38*(3–4), 403–432.

Kor, Y. Y., Mahoney, J. T., & Michael, S. C. (2007). Resources, capabilities and entrepreneurial perceptions. *Journal of Management Studies, 44*(7), 1187–1212.

Lavie, D., & Rosenkopf, L. (2006). Balancing exploration and exploitation in alliance formation. *Academy of Management Journal, 49*(4), 797–818.

Leana, C. R., & Barry, B. (2000). Stability and change as simultaneous experiences in organizational life. *Academy of Management Review, 25*(4), 753–759.

Lee, N. (2014). What holds back high-growth firms? Evidence from UK SMEs. *Small Business Economics, 43*, 183–195.

Leiserowitz, A. A., Kates, R. W., & Parris, T. M. (2006). Sustainability values, attitudes, and behaviors: A review of multinational and global trends. *Annual Review of Environmental Resources, 31*(1), 413–444.

Leiter, K. (1980). A primer on ethnomethodology. New York: Oxford University Press.

Levie, J., & Lichtenstein, B. B. (2010). A terminal assessment of stages theory: Introducing a dynamic states approach to entrepreneurship. *Entrepreneurship Theory and Practice, 34*(2), 317–350.

Levinthal, D. A. (1997). Adaptation on rugged landscapes. *Management Science, 43*(7), 934–950.

Lewis, M. W. (2000). Exploring paradox: Toward a more comprehensive guide. *Academy of Management Review, 25*(4), 760–776.

Lewis, M. W., & Smith, W. K. (2014). Paradox as a metatheoretical perspective: Sharpening the focus and widening the scope. *Journal of Applied Behavioral Science, 50*(2), 127–179.

Lewis, M. W., Welsh, M. A., Dehler, G. E., & Green, S. G. (2002). Product development tensions: Exploring contrasting styles of project management. *Academy of Management Journal, 45*(3), 546–564.

Lichtenstein, B. B., Carter, N. M., Dooley, K. J., & Gartner, W. B. (2007). Complexity dynamics of nascent entrepreneurship. *Journal of Business Venturing, 22*(2), 236–261.

Lin, H. E., & McDonough III, E. F. (2011). Investigating the role of leadership and organizational culture in fostering innovation ambidexterity. *IEEE Transactions on Engineering Management, 58*(3), 497–509.

Louis, M. R. (1983). Surprise and sense making: What newcomers experience in entering unfamiliar organizational settings. *Journal of Library Administration, 4*(1), 95–123.

Lubatkin, M. H., Simsek, Z., Ling, Y., & Veiga, J. F. (2006). Ambidexterity and performance in small-to medium-sized firms: The pivotal role of top management team behavioral integration. *Journal of Management, 32*(5), 646–672.

Lüscher, L. S., & Lewis, M. W. (2008). Organizational change and managerial sensemaking: Working through paradox. *Academy of Management Journal, 51*(2), 221–240.

Maitlis, S., & Christianson, M. (2014). Sensemaking in organizations: Taking stock and moving forward. *Academy of Management Annals, 8*(1), 57–125.

Maitlis, S., & Lawrence, T. B. (2007). Triggers and enablers of sensegiving in organizations. *Academy of Management Journal, 50*(1), 57–84.

Maitlis, S., & Sonenshein, S. (2010). Sensemaking in crisis and change: Inspiration and insights from Weick (1988). *Journal of Management Studies, 47*(3), 551–580.

Makri, M., & Scandura, T. A. (2010). Exploring the effects of creative CEO leadership on innovation in high-technology firms. *The Leadership Quarterly, 21*(1), 75–88.

Marquis, C., & Battilana, J. (2009). Acting globally but thinking locally? The enduring influence of local communities on organizations. *Research in Organizational Behavior, 29*, 283–302.

Merkus, S., de Heer, J., & Veenswijk, M. (2014). Framing the zone: Political executives engaging in a narrative-framing contest during strategic decision-making. *Planning Practice & Research, 5*(29), 569–584.

Merkus, S., Willems, T., Schipper, D., van Marrewijk, A., Koppenjan, J., Veenswijk, M., & Bakker, H. (2017). A storm is coming? Collective sensemaking and ambiguity in an inter-organizational team managing railway system disruptions. *Journal of Change Management, 17*(3), 228–248.

Mintzberg, H., Ahlstrand, B., & Lampel, J. (2001). *Strategy safari: A guided tour through the wilds of strategic management.* New York: The Free Press.

Miron-Spektor, E., Erez, M., & Naveh, E. (2004). Do personal characteristics and cultural values that promote innovation, quality, and efficiency compete or complement each other? *Journal of Organizational Behavior, 25*(2), 175–199.

Miron-Spektor, E., Erez, M., & Naveh, E. (2011). The effect of conformist and attentive-to-detail members on team innovation: Reconciling the innovation paradox. *Academy of Management Journal, 54*(4), 740–760.

Miron-Spektor, E., & Erez, M. (2017). Looking at creativity through a paradox lens. In W. K. Smith, M. W. Lewis, P. Jarzabkowski, & A. Langley (Eds.), The Oxford handbook of organizational paradox (pp. 434–451). New York: Oxford University Press.

Mom, T. J., Chang, Y. Y., Cholakova, M., & Jansen, J. J. (2019). A multilevel integrated framework of firm HR practices, individual ambidexterity, and organizational ambidexterity. *Journal of Management, 45*(7), 3009–3034.

Mom, T. J., Van den Bosch, F. A., & Volberda, H. W. (2007). Investigating managers' exploration and exploitation activities: The influence of top-down, bottom-up, and horizontal knowledge inflows. *Journal of Management Studies, 44*(6), 910–931.

Morgeson, F. P., DeRue, D. S., & Karam, E. P. (2009). Leadership in teams: A functional approach to understanding leadership structures and processes. *Journal of Management, 36*(1), 5–39.

Mu, T., Van Riel, A., & Schouteten, R. (2022). Individual ambidexterity in SMEs: Towards a typology aligning the concept, antecedents and outcomes. *Journal of Small Business Management, 60*(2), 347–378.

Mueller, S., Volery, T., & Von Siemens, B. (2012). What do entrepreneurs actually do? An observational study of entrepreneurs' everyday behavior in the start–up and growth stages. *Entrepreneurship Theory and Practice, 36*(5), 995–1017.

Muñoz, P., & Cohen, B. (2018). Entrepreneurial narratives in sustainable venturing: Beyond people, profit, and planet. *Journal of Small Business Management, 56*(S1), 154–176.

Murnighan, J. K., & Conlon, D. E. (1991). The dynamics of intense work groups: A study of British string quartets. *Administrative Science Quarterly, 36*(2), 165–186.

Nemanich, L. A., & Vera, D. (2009). Transformational leadership and ambidexterity in the context of an acquisition. The Leadership Quarterly, 20(1), 19–33.

Nicholls-Nixon, C. L. (2005). Rapid growth and high performance: The entrepreneur's "impossible dream?" *Academy of Management Perspectives, 19*(1), 77–89.

Nord, W. R. (1978). Dreams of humanization and the realities of power. *Academy of Management Review, 3*(3), 674–679.

Ocasio, W., Loewenstein, J., & Nigam, A. (2015). How streams of communication reproduce and change institutional logics: The role of categories. *Academy of Management Review, 40*(1), 28–48.

O'Reilly III, C. A., & Tushman, M. L. (2013). Organizational ambidexterity: Past, present, and future. *Academy of Management Perspectives, 27*(4), 324–338.

Papachroni, A., Heracleous, L., & Paroutis, S. (2015). Organizational ambidexterity through the lens of paradox theory: Building a novel research agenda. *The Journal of Applied Behavioral Science, 51*(1), 71–93.

Parrish, B. D. (2010). Sustainability-driven entrepreneurship: Principles of organization design. *Journal of Business Venturing, 25*(5), 510–523.

Patriotta, G. (2003a). Sensemaking on the shop floor: Narratives of knowledge in organizations. *Journal of Management Studies, 40*(2), 349–375.

Patriotta, G., & Brown, A. D. (2011). Sensemaking, metaphors and performance evaluation. *Scandinavian Journal of Management, 27*(1), 34–43.

Pfeffer, J. (1981). Management as symbolic action: The creation and maintenance of organizational paradigm. *Research in Organizational Behavior, 3*, 1–52.

Poole, M. S., & Van de Ven, A. H. (1989). Using paradox to build management and organization theories. *Academy of Management Review, 14*(4), 562–578.

Poole, M. S., & Van de Ven, A. H. (Eds.) (2004). *Handbook of organizational change and innovation.* Oxford: Oxford University Press.

Poole, M. S., & Van de Ven, A. H. (2010). Empirical methods for research on organizational decision-making processes. In D. J. Koehler & N. Harvey (Eds.), *The Blackwell handbook of decision making,* Malden: Balckwell Publishing (pp. 543–580).

Pratt, M. G., & Rafaeli, A. (1997). Organizational dress as a symbol of multilayered social identities. *Academy of Management Journal, 40*(4), 862–898.

Probst, G., Raisch, S., & Tushman, M. L. (2011). Ambidextrous leadership: Emerging challenges for business and HR leaders. *Organizational Dynamics, 40*(4), 326–334.

Quinn, R. (1984). Applying the competing values approach to leadership: Toward an integrative model. In J. G. Hunt, R. Steward, C. Schriesheim, & D. Hosking (Eds.), *Leaders and managers: International perspectives on managerial behavior and leadership* (pp. 10–27). New York: Paragon.

Raisch, S., & Birkinshaw, J. (2008). Organizational ambidexterity: Antecedents, outcomes, and moderators. *Journal of Management, 34*(3), 375–409.

Raisch, S., Birkinshaw, J., Probst, G., & Tushman, M. (2009). Organizational ambidexterity: Balancing and exploitation and exploration for sustained performance. *Organization Science, 20*(4), 685–695.

Raisch, S., & Zimmerman, A. (2017). Pathways to ambidexterity: A process perspective on the exploration–exploitation paradox. In W. K. Smith, M. W. Lewis, P. Jarzabkowski, & A. Langley (Eds.), *The Oxford handbook of organizational paradox* (pp. 315–336). Oxford: Oxford University Press.

Rosing, K., Frese, M., & Bausch, A. (2011). Explaining the heterogeneity of the leadership-innovation relationship: Ambidextrous leadership. *The Leadership Quarterly, 22*(5), 956–974.

Rosing, K., Rosenbusch, N., & Frese, M. (2010). Ambidextrous leadership in the innovation process. *Innovation and International Corporate Growth,* In A. Gerybadze, U. Hommel, H.W. Reiners & D. Thomaschewski (eds) (pp.191–204). berlin: Springer.

Rosing, K., & Zacher, H. (2017). Individual ambidexterity: The duality of exploration and exploitation and its relationship with innovative performance. *European Journal of Work and Organizational Psychology, 26*(5), 694–709.

Rouleau, L., & Balogun, J. (2011). Middle managers, strategic sensemaking, and discursive competence. *Journal of Management Studies, 48*(5), 953–983.

Sandberg, J., & Tsoukas, H. (2015). 'Making sense of the sensemaking perspective: Its constituents, limitations, and opportunities for further development. *Journal of Organizational Behavior, 36*(1), 6–S32.

Sarasvathy SD (2001) Causation and effectuation: Toward a theoretical shift from economic inevitability to entrepreneurial contingency. *Academy of Management Review, 26*, 243–263.

Schad, J., Lewis, M. W., Raisch, S., & Smith, W. K. (2016). Paradox research in management science: Looking back to move forward. *The Academy of Management Annals, 10*(1), 5–64.

Schaltegger, S., & Wagner, M. (2011). Sustainable entrepreneurship and sustainability innovation: Categories and interactions. *Business Strategy and the Environment, 20*(4), 222–237.

Scherer, A. G., Palazzo, G., & Seidl, D. (2013). Managing legitimacy in complex and heterogeneous environments: Sustainable development in a globalized world. *Journal of Management Studies, 50*, 259–284.

Sheep, M. L., Fairhurst, G. T., & Khazanchi, S. (2017). Knots in the discourse of innovation: Investigating multiple tensions in a required spin-off. *Organization Studies, 38*(3–4), 463–488.

Shepherd, D. A., & Patzelt, H. (2021). *Entrepreneurial strategy: Starting, managing, and scaling new ventures.* Cham: Springer Nature.

Shepherd, D. A., & Patzelt, H. (2022). A call for research on the scaling of organizations and the scaling of social impact. *Entrepreneurship Theory and Practice 46*(2), 255–268.

Siggelkow, N., & Levinthal, D. A. (2003). Temporarily divide to conquer: Centralized, decentralized, and reintegrated organizational approaches to exploration and adaptation. Organization Science, 14(6), 650–669.

Silva, T., Cunha, M. P. E., Clegg, S. R., Neves, P., Rego, A., & Rodrigues, R. A. (2014). Smells like team spirit: Opening a paradoxical black box. *Human Relations, 67*(3), 287–310.

Simsek, Z., Heavey, C., & Fox, B. C. (2018). Interfaces of strategic leaders: A conceptual framework, review, and research agenda. *Journal of Management, 44*(1), 280–324.

Simsek, Z., Jansen, J. J., Minichilli, A., & Escriba-Esteve, A. (2015). Strategic leadership and leaders in entrepreneurial contexts: A nexus for innovation and impact missed? *Journal of Management Studies, 52*(4), 463–478.

Slawinski, N., & Bansal, P. (2012). A matter of time: The temporal perspectives of organizational responses to climate change. Organization Studies, 33(11), 1537–1563.

Smith, W. K. (2014). Dynamic decision making: A model of senior leaders managing strategic paradoxes. *Academy of Management Journal, 57*(6), 1592–1623.

Smith, W. K., Besharov, M. L., Wessels, A. K., & Chertok, M. (2012). A paradoxical leadership model for social entrepreneurs: Challenges, leadership skills, and pedagogical tools for managing social and commercial demands. *Academy of Management, 11*(3), 463–478.

Smith, W. K., Binns, A., & Tushman, M. L. (2010). Complex business models: Managing strategic paradoxes simultaneously. *Long Range Planning, 43*(2), 448–461.

Smith, W. K., Gonin, M., & Besharov, M. L. (2013). Managing social-business tensions: A review and research agenda for social enterprise. *Business Ethics Quarterly, 23*(3), 407–442.

Smith, W. K., & Lewis, M. W. (2011). Toward a theory of paradox: A dynamic equilibrium model of organizing. Academy of Management Review, 36(2), 381–403.

Smith, W. K., & Tushman, M. L. (2005). Managing strategic contradictions: A top management model for managing innovation streams. Organization Science, 16(5), 522–536.

Snehvrat, S., Kumar, A., Kumar, R., & Dutta, S. (2018). The state of ambidexterity research: A data mining approach. *International Journal of Organizational Analysis, 26*(2), 343–367.

Sparr, J. L. (2018). Paradoxes in organizational change: The crucial role of leaders' sensegiving. *Journal of Change Management, 18*(22), 162–180.

Stein, M. (2004). The critical period of disasters: Insights from sense-making and psychoanalytic theory. *Human Relations, 57*(10), 1243–1261.

Stigliani, I., & Ravasi, D. (2012) Organizing thoughts and connecting brains: Material practices and the transition from individual to group-level prospective sensemaking. *Academy of Management Journal, 55*(5), 1232–1259.

Strang, D., & Meyer, J. W. (1993). Institutional conditions for diffusion. *Theory and Society, 22*(4), 487–511.

Tempelaar, M. P., & Rosenkranz, N. A. (2019). Switching hats: The effect of role transition on individual ambidexterity. *Journal of Management, 45*(4), 1517–1539.

Thompson, J. D. (1967). *Organizations in action: Social science bases of administrative theory.* New Jersey: Transaction Publishers.

Thornton, P. H., Ocasio, W., & Lounsbury, M. (2012). *The institutional logics perspective: A new approach to culture, structure, and process.* Oxford: Oxford University Press on Demand.

Tuan Luu, T. (2017). Ambidextrous leadership, entrepreneurial orientation, and operational performance: Organizational social capital as a moderator. *Leadership & Organization Development Journal, 38*(2), 229–253.

Tushman, M. L., & O'Reilly III, C. A. (1996). Ambidextrous organizations: Managing evolutionary and revolutionary change. California Management Review, 38(4), 8–29.

Vaara, E., Sonenshein, S., & Boje, D. (2016). Narratives as sources of stability and change in organizations: Approaches and directions for future research. *The Academy of Management Annals, 10*(1), 495–560.

Vaara, E., & Tienari, J. (2011). On the narrative construction of multinational corporations: An antenarrative analysis of legitimation and resistance in a cross-border merger. *Organization Science, 22*(2), 370–390.

Van den Bosch, F. A., Volberda, H. W., & De Boer, M. (1999). Coevolution of firm absorptive capacity and knowledge environment: Organizational forms and combinative capabilities. *Organization Science, 10*(5), 551–568.

Van der Byl, C. A., & Slawinski, N. (2015). Embracing tensions in corporate sustainability: A review of research from win-wins and trade-offs to paradoxes and beyond. *Organization & Environment, 28*(1), 54–79.

Venkatraman, N., Lee, C. H., & Iyer, B. (2007). Strategic ambidexterity and sales growth: A longitudinal test in the software sector. *Unpublished manuscript (earlier version presented at the Academy of Management Meetings, 2005).*

Vera, D., & Crossan, M. (2004). Strategic leadership and organizational learning. *Academy of Management Review, 29*(2), 222–240.

Vlaar, P. W., Van den Bosch, F. A., & Volberda, H. W. (2006). Coping with problems of understanding in interorganizational relationships: Using formalization as a means to make sense. *Organization Studies, 27*(11), 1617–1638.

Vlaar, P. W., Van Fenema, P. C., & Tiwari, V. (2008). Cocreating understanding and value in distributed work: How members of onsite and offshore vendor teams give, make, demand, and break sense. *MIS Quarterly, 32*(2), 227–255.

Weick, K. E. (1979). *The social psychology of organizing* (2nd ed.). New York: McGraw-Hill.

Weick, K. E. (1995). *Sensemaking in organizations* (vol. 3). New York: Sage.

Weick, K. E. (2009). *Making sense of the organization: The impermanent organization.* Chichester: John Wiley & Sons Ltd.

Weick, K. E., & Roberts, K. H. (1993). Collective mind in organizations: Heedful inter-relating on flight decks. *Administrative Science Quarterly, 38*(3), 357–381.

Weick, K. E., Sutcliffe, K. M., & Obstfeld, D. (2005). Organizing and the process of sensemaking. *Organization Science, 16*(4), 409–421.

Wolbers, J., & Boersma, K. (2013). The common operational picture as collective sensemaking. *Journal of Contingencies and Crisis Management, 21*(4), 186–199.

Yeganegi, S., Laplume, A. O., Dass, P., & Greidanus, N. S. (2019). Individual-level ambidexterity and entrepreneurial entry. *Journal of Small Business Management, 57*(4), 1444–1463.

Zahra, S. A., Sapienza, H. J., & Davidsson, P. (2006). Entrepreneurship and dynamic capabilities: A review, model and research agenda. *Journal of Management Studies, 43*(4), 917–955.

3 How the research was conducted

The case study method to explore innovation in action

OVERVIEW

This chapter outlines the methodology utilised in the research to reveal the value of the in-depth study.

A *qualitative case study methodology* was selected to observe natural sensemaking dynamics in response to innovation demands. Rather than trying to observe several different cases, the decision was made to focus on a single case that could provide greater depth rather than breadth. The case organisation was therefore specifically selected through a purposive sampling approach, which enabled a targeted study of an innovative purpose-driven organisation in action. To gain deep insights and minimise the risk of potential unnatural external researcher interference, the approach involved some ethnographic immersion. As a 'participant observer', the researcher was then able to experience the working of the organisation at a number of different levels and to take more of a 'fly on the wall' perspective.

Data collection consisted of reading through relevant documentation (such as reports, website and marketing materials, policies etc); making field notes based on observations of staff in action; recording and transcribing formal and informal interviews with all members of the senior leadership team and selected other staff and clients; and using the 'draw and talk' technique to help individuals more easily express their thoughts and feelings during the interview process.

The transcripts and notes were then run through data analysis software, which assisted with the identification and organisation of the key trends and themes through coding. Analysing metaphors, in particular, also helped to reveal some more nuanced underlying themes. Finally, a detailed event history timeline was constructed to weave the independent elements together and gain a bigger picture view on how the dynamics developed over time.

DOI: 10.4324/9781003426691-3

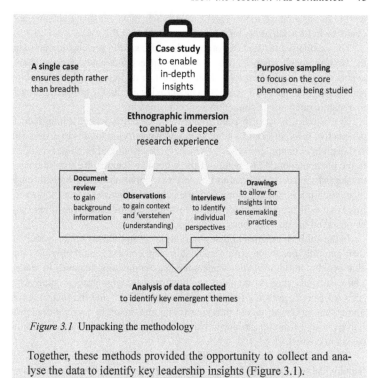

Figure 3.1 Unpacking the methodology

Together, these methods provided the opportunity to collect and ana-lyse the data to identify key leadership insights (Figure 3.1).

Discovering sensemaking practices through case studies

Several different qualitative methods have typically been used to study sense-making (such as case studies, ethnographies and textual analysis drawing on qualitative data, including interviews, observations and archival data), and multiple data sources are usually recommended.[1] Elements of all of these methods were utilised in this study as part of the overall case study methodology.

You might quite reasonably be wondering what the value of a case study is and how a single case study can be useful in examining phenomenon like this. A case study is 'an empirical inquiry that investigates a contemporary phenomenon (the case) in depth and within its real-world context'.[2] Case stud-ies have been identified as ideal for observing senior leadership practices in context.[3] and they enable the analysis of the intersection between empirical evidence, which is often complex and unique,[4] and theoretical ideas, which can be abstract and tentative. While empirical evidence allows us to explore and articulate theories,[5] theoretical ideas provide a means for interpreting the world.[6] In this context, theory can be used to help make sense of evidence, and evidence in turn can assist with focusing and refining theory.

The qualitative methods incorporated in case studies are considered to be the best approach when there is a need to understand states, processes and events directly, and when there is an interest in finding causal relationships and looking for specific outcomes.[7] They provide a valuable holistic approach to dynamic phenomena studied in a specific context.[8]

Case studies have also been found to be effective where a longitudinal perspective is required and where the researcher is trying to 'observe, describe and explain dynamic processes... which are best captured in close proximity to the phenomenon.'[9] The nature of these tensions, emanating from the need to take risks, push boundaries and explore new opportunities for breakthrough innovation (exploration), along with the need to maintain systems and structures that will support incremental innovation (exploitation), can often only be observed in situ over time.

In the study, I anticipated that observations of individual senior leaders in their naturally occurring senior leadership team contexts could provide valuable insights into how senior leaders navigate competing demands in teams. The case study process included an 'opportunistic ethnography' approach[10] 'derived from... personal interests and backgrounds',[11] and the focus was on immersion, observation and interviews. The immersion in a single organisation over an 18-month period, in particular, enabled the observation of processes in context.

As sensemaking has been identified as a means of tapping into underlying paradoxical tensions, the focus in the case study was on how senior leaders make sense of the experiences of and responses to tensions emerging from competing innovation demands. The corroboration of this observation data with interview data transcribed from repeated interviews with the senior leadership team members and other individuals in the organisation then helped to provide multiple perspectives on the emergent episodes and storylines in order to weave together a coherent narrative.

Understanding the research that had already been done in this area helped to prepare for the immersive in-depth case study determined that the case study methodology could provide the opportunity to observe what individual leaders bring to the team context and how they negotiate differences to reach consensus. I realised that exploring how individual senior leaders negotiate their own personal biases in relation to other team members, as well as how the senior leadership team as a whole agrees to move forward,[12] could lead to a better understanding of how purpose-driven innovation could be navigated.[13] This involved investigating how a shared sense of meaning is negotiated[14] and how coordinated action between senior leaders is facilitated.[15]

The research design therefore relied on a qualitative methodology based on an inductive approach. Rather than coming to the organisation with set ideas and hypothesis to test, the chosen approach instead required observing and exploring day-to-day actions and practices to see what insights emerged.

The benefit of a single in-depth case study

There has been a particular focus in the literature on the value of in-depth case studies for providing rich insights into an area that is being studied.[16] In this study, I decided to focus on a single case to explore leadership sensemaking in depth. This provided an opportunity to really go deep into the subject rather than trying to cover breadth through analysing multiple cases.

Cases are dynamic and the process of casing can adapt to emerging evidence and theory connections, particularly where there are a small number of cases or single cases. 'Theoretical framework, empirical fieldwork, and case analysis evolve simultaneously' through a research approach that has been identified as 'systematic combining'.[17] This approach involves matching theory with reality, along with direction and redirection as the process evolves.

In-depth single case studies have also been found to be useful for inductive theory building or for starting with the exploration of an emergent phenomenon rather than with preconceived hypotheses. This is especially important when the phenomena being explored is relatively new and during the early stages of research in a new field.[18]

The case study approach employed for this research provided the opportunity for an in-depth analysis of the senior leadership sensemaking processes in the one organisation, resulting in rich insights. Rather than taking a variable-oriented approach to theorising, in which general laws are sought after extracting and deconstructing the key elements,[19] the focus on a specific single case organisation in a specific context allowed for a more holistic approach.[20] The in-depth case study consisted of a combination of interviews and observations along with some analysis of internal documentary material such as annual reports, strategy documents, and internal communications – as well as external documentation such as press releases, brochures and website materials. Table 3.1 covers in more detail the methodological approach for collecting data for the case study.

The single case study enables deep insights into individual experiences[21] by showing the interplay between ideas and evidence, as 'empirical accounts are brought into conjunction with theoretical ideas and an account of the context of the study, and together they produce a trustworthy narrative from the research'.[22] Yet there are both advantages and challenges of going in depth with a single case organisation. These include the challenges of balancing proximity and distance,[23] balancing the role of actor

Table 3.1 Methodology summary for in-depth case study

Profile of organisation selected

Key details of the case organisation 'Social Support Organisation' (SSO) :

- Established in 2001.
- Provides services to support migrants and people seeking asylum.
- Includes innovation as a core value and offers more than 30 highly innovative programs.
- Encompasses both for-profit (social enterprise) and not-for-profit functions.
- Had recently been through a period of rapid growth resulting in a crisis with the departure of directors and a number of other staff.

Details of methodology

Data collection Included:

- Document review: 50+ internal and external facing documents (including business plans, internal comms, advertising and websites)
- Ethnographic immersion: Spending extended periods of time in the organisation to enable a deeper and richer experience of relevant phenomenon
- Participatory and non-participatory observations: Both participatory and non-participatory observation approaches over an 18-month period to facilitate deeper insights
- Extended formal and informal interviews:
  o Open-ended interviews with senior leadership team members (2×9 at the beginning and towards the end of the research period) plus with other members of the organisation (20)
  o Approximately 60–100 mins for senior leadership team members, 30–60 mins for others
  o 59 interviews in total, including 28 formal and 31 informal interviews
  o Asked individuals to describe their personal experiences of the impact of organisation innovation and growth over time
  o The 'draw and talk' technique was also included for final interviews with the senior leadership team

---

and observer,[24] and being a neutral outsider versus representing headquarters.[25] Ultimately, this approach to research is known to provide the most in-depth insights.

Looking for causal processes that lead to specific outcomes in particular contexts can enable a broader understanding of the issues explored. Rather than attempting to research multiple cases in order to lead to analytical generalisation, the more classic single case study can provide insights into the dynamics. A natural generalisation can evolve through social reflection on personal experiences.[26] The outcome of a case study like this may not be a single, convergent explanation but rather the uncovering of diverse 'emic meanings held by the people within the case',[27] so representing the multiplicity of perspectives is important in this methodology. An emergent logic was followed to acknowledge that the research question and boundaries of the case could coevolve as the research progressed.[28]

I recognised that observing the sensemaking process in action would help to identify potential paradoxical tensions as they arose and the case approach would also ensure that I would be able to identify and accept the innate elasticity of the processes and be open to whatever outcomes would emerge.[29]

The importance of ethnographic immersion

Well-known anthropologist Branislav Malinowski lived amongst the Trobriand Islanders for many years from 1914. During that time, he learned the language and was then able to report on the social, legal and economic systems from more of an insider perspective. This methodological approach to research represents deep ethnographic immersion.

The in-depth case study in this research also involved some ethnographic immersion, as ethnography has been identified as being the most effective means for gaining insights into cultural phenomena at the micro level.[30] The specific approach to the case study research was a form of 'opportunistic ethnography',[31] which has been more common in sociology than in management. This refers to studies emerging from a form of group membership 'derived from... personal interests and backgrounds'.[32] In ethnographic research, interactions between individuals in a specific organisational context over the long term can reveal the foundations for group-level phenomenon, which in turn shape organisational culture.[33] Positivist approaches, or research approaches that start with a preconceived hypothesis to test, are not appropriate for capturing cultural complexity at this level. An inductive ethnographic approach like a case study, on the other hand, provides the opportunity to more accurately focus on the intricacies.[34] Ethnography can lead to the development of clear constructs, which in turn can assist with advancing and testing theory.[35]

Although this research did not involve a more rigorous form of ethnographic immersion, it still required participatory observation, which necessitates periods of strategic involvement. The emergent theories were developed from the outcomes of observation of the sensemaking process. The act of observing and interpreting individual behaviours and team interactions in the case study context was in itself a sensemaking process to 'understand and give meaning to the unfolding of events and actions taken over time'.[36] The data was collected in situ through an active research process, rather than relying on secondary data collection.

Some of the case study methods used in this study included discourse analysis and micro-ethnography, which enabled the exploration of the sensemaking processes in real time.[37] This provided the opportunity to observe and analyse process data and 'understand how and why events play out over time'.[38] The advantage of combining different data sources in a case study is 'the development of converging lines of inquiry' which enhances the construct validity of the study.[39] The analysis of the data collected involved an iterative interplay between the identification of the initial theoretical framework from the early literature review prior to the research phase, the data that emerged during the research phase itself and more in-depth studies of the literature based on the emerging data from the research phase itself.

The value of purposive sampling

In some research designs, the selection of participants or 'sampling' needs to be random, such as when there is an experimental intervention that needs to be compared to a control group. In this in-depth case, however, the sampling was 'purposive'. In this study, I specifically set out to select an innovative and growing not-for-profit organisation that was currently experiencing tensions in implementing innovation to gain an insight into innovation leadership practices. Purposive cases are useful because of their uniqueness, rather than due to their representativeness, and the case was chosen due to the salience of the attributes being explored.[40] As the specific phenomena are highlighted in the case organisation, it was identified that it should be possible to more easily view and theorise about the phenomena.

Media reports at the time the study started indicated that the targeted case organisation clearly exhibited tensions from attempts at purpose-driven innovation. As a not-for-profit with a hybrid component, I expected that this organisation would also be subject to resource limitations and plurality,[41] along with tension between a focus on purpose while also ensuring sustainability and capacity.[42] The organisation was seeking to pursue socially and sustainable innovation practices while simultaneously meeting economic imperatives.[43]

This selection of an information-rich case was deliberate to allow for a specific focus on the challenges being studied. Gaining an in-depth knowledge of an organisation can help to ensure the context is being adequately considered and interpretations are more accurate. Single case studies like this can 'illustrate conceptual frameworks and highlight the need for new lenses to explore phenomena'.[44] This helped to clarify meaning by enabling an observation of the phenomena through identifying different realities and enabling them to be seen from multiple perspectives.[45]

The techniques that enable in-depth insights

In the single in-depth case study explored here, a number of methodological techniques were used to help gain the in-depth insights.

Some of these are fairly standard for qualitative research, including observations of the senior leadership teams and the staff at work, along with both formal and informal interviews to identify deeper motivations. Other techniques are more unusual, including asking senior leadership team members to represent their thoughts and feelings in drawings, to assist with ensuring there were not the standard limitations that speech might impose and that some more creative perspectives might emerge.

A key opportunity for observations came from observing senior leadership team meetings in action. The senior leadership team of seven directors plus the chief executive officer (CEO) and Chief Operating Officer (COO) met weekly for two hours to discuss projects and make strategic decisions. At the time of the research, they were discussing how to proceed with the new catering and cleaning enterprises and were planning to make business plans for them, specifically considering whether the focus should be on the social purpose or ensuring the businesses were profitable. This particular issue was being explored in relation to the general organisation strategy as well, and there were questions around whether the approach they decided on should become a model for the organisation as a whole. The director team was concerned that the group had not yet had enough time to make strategic decisions around this issue, and it had become a source of tension for the senior leadership team. This issue therefore provided an area of focus for observation.

A research journal was kept throughout this period with summaries of research opportunities and details of general and specific observations of both formal and informal events. The journal was regularly reviewed throughout the research period to provide insights from emerging data and to define the iterative literature review process and develop directions for the research.

Document review

An initial document review of more than 50 internal documents (including business plans and internal communications) and external facing documents (such as advertising brochures, websites and media reports) provided valuable background information and insights into the formal and informal messages, structures and relationships within the organisation.

Observations

Observations were made of general work activities and of these naturally occurring senior leader meetings. Observations are an important part of the case study approach as 'the detailed observations entailed in the case study method enable us to study many different aspects, examine them in relation to each other, view the process within its total environment and also use the researchers' capacity for '*verstehen*' (understanding)'.[46]

Observations assist with the theory building process as they rely on 'past literature and empirical observation or experience as well as on the insight of the theorist to build incrementally more powerful theories'.[47] As in other case study research on senior managers' sensemaking in response to change,[48]

I had the opportunity to observe multiple senior meetings and workshops over the 18-month period in regular monthly visits for up to a week at a time. Other general relevant naturally occurring events observed included staff meetings, workshops and events (such as special budgeting meetings, scenario planning meetings, staff development days, department workshops and events for members). Data was eventually collected from a total of 23 meetings.

After some unofficial informal visits, the research period officially started when the COO arrived in the role and came to a natural closure at the end of the research period when the COO moved into a new position. During this time, the senior team essentially remained the same, with the new director of fundraising arriving six months into the research period, the director of business services going on maternity leave towards the end of the research period and the second humanitarian services director departing at the end of the research period (to take up a GM role in another organisation).

Both participatory and non-participatory observation approaches were utilised,[49] including some volunteer work in administration in the organisation's Innovation Hub. I regularly spent time immersed in a volunteer capacity in the 'Innovation Hub', assisting for up to several days per month with tasks such as reception of guests and preparing documentation to support the Hub Director. This enabled an insider's perspective on the day-to-day running of the organisation, including exposure to casual conversations and behaviours.

Balancing the role of actor and observer can be challenging where the researcher needs to stress objectivity in the observation process as occurred in this case process. When the researcher is spending a lot of time in the organisation, they will typically be asked for their opinions, particularly in the feedback process. Even interviewing is a form of intervention as it sends signals to participants that an area is of particular interest in the research, and asking interview questions can impact affective and cognitive processes. I therefore tried to ensure the impact was minimised where possible by compartmentalising the research through providing feedback only after the primary research had been conducted.

Interviews

The interviews included in the research were designed to help to identify different perspectives through asking individuals to describe their personal experiences and attitudes related to the impact of organisation innovation and growth over time.

The interviews involved 'retrospectively assembled narrative sensemaking constructions'[50] or descriptions from memory of events and individual interpretations of these events. This process enabled recognition of the variety of 'modes' of discourse that contribute to sensemaking[51] rather than solely relying on verbal descriptions and written text.[52] Questioning each of the individuals in the senior leadership team through interviews helped them to recount experiences related to the relevant context.[53] Each of the individual responses could then be seen as fragments that were not single data points, but rather more in-depth narratives that could illuminate experiences.[54]

The interviews were semi-structured, meaning that while some core questions were established prior to the interviews, I anticipated that each interview could evolve differently according to individual needs and preferences. I expected that having more of a discussion format could help ensure there was the opportunity for interviewees to move in any direction into any area as relevant. Semi-structured interviews acknowledge that important details can emerge not only from following the interviewer's intended line of enquiry but also through providing a more relaxed environment that enables open interpretation and exploration outside of the anticipated boundaries.[55] The naturally evolving dialogue between the interviewer and the interviewee was embraced as it empowers the participant to become involved in the knowledge production or co-creation of the process itself rather than being a passive recipient.[56]

Two semi-structured formal face-to-face interviews were conducted with the senior leadership team members at the beginning and towards the end of this period, involving discussions with the full current senior leadership team of nine directors (including the CEO) for approximately 60–100 minutes each. Semi-structured interviews of 30–60 minutes were also conducted with more than 20 managers and staff at other levels of the organisation to provide perspectives on the impact of senior leadership team strategies and decisions.

A total of 28 formal and 31 informal interviews (59 in total) were conducted with employees in general, including with staff in the 'Innovation Hub' which was the focus of innovative development for the organisation, and additionally with some client members. All of the formal interviews were audio recorded and transcribed, and notes were taken by the researcher during or following all the formal and informal discussions. In this case, meaning rather than frequency was important in determining the overall theme and the number of interviews was less relevant.[57] The aim of the interviews was to identify collective sensemaking strategies senior leaders might use when dealing with paradoxes in this context, which provided the opportunity to identify the different individual and group perspectives.

Drawings

When the final interviews of up to 60 minutes were conducted with each of the nine senior leadership team members towards the end of the research period, a 'draw and talk' technique was used.[58] The 'draw and talk' technique involves asking interviewees to answer the interviewer's questions in a pictorial format and to describe what they are drawing as they create the images.[59] Drawings can provide greater penetration into the interview data by enabling contextualisation, ensuring focus, exemplifying core principles and allowing for reflexivity.[60]

Drawings have relatively recently been used in management and organisation studies as a method of data collection when studying sensitive or difficult-to-access topics, such as emotional responses to change,[61] identity and culture[62] and management learning.[63] This technique is a recognised variation to the established verbal interview approach,[64] as drawing has been identified as a useful way of understanding the sensemaking practices people in organisations use to work through the paradoxical tensions and consolidate responses.[65]

Asking interview participants to draw what they are experiencing as part of the interview process can bypass potential verbal boundaries and limitations and allow for a broader exploration of emotions and practices,[66] leading to greater honesty.[67] Additionally, pictures can reveal a different narrative to what is verbalised.[68] The 'draw and talk' technique was included in this study to help identify how team members perceived the relationships within the executive team. Although the role of discourse in making sense of these tensions has been studied extensively, the potential role of drawing as a tool for assisting with surfacing latent tensions as part of the sensemaking process has yet to be explored in detail, so it was anticipated this element might provide some interesting additional insights.

For this visual construction component, the participants were asked to draw their perceptions of the executive team (including executive team dynamics) in the present and past, along with what they thought would be an ideal state for the future. They were also asked to describe and draw what actions they thought might need to be taken to reach the ideal future state.

This 'draw and talk' technique enabled retrospective sensemaking[69] through allowing for the variety of 'modes' of discourse that contribute to sensemaking[70] rather than solely relying on verbal discourse and written text.[71] The 'draw and talk' method included questions covering topics such as:

1 How the individual perceived the leadership team was functioning at the start of the research period
2 How the individual perceived the leadership team was currently functioning
3 What they identified as the ideal future leadership team
4 How they thought the ideal future leadership team could be achieved
5 How they would depict their own personal journey over their time with the organisation

How the data collected was analysed

The analysis of the qualitative data collected from the case study included three stages[72]:

1 **Reading and coding textual material** (documents and interview transcripts) through identifying 'nodal points' or key emergent concepts related to stories, narratives and discourses

2 **Re-analysing the initial coding** and organising the data around dominant themes and categories
3 **Exploring the broader 'genres' or 'themes' and 'plots'** – including how individuals represented themselves and their positions, and how the broader depictions of their lives could be represented

The case study approach to research can be challenging as it can be difficult to work with a 'soft' approach.[73] Cases can be perceived as 'meaningful but complex configurations of events and structures',[74] and this methodology aims to identify theoretical implications from complex problems through an iterative theory building approach.[75] Yet the inherent complex nature of the case study makes it difficult to achieve these intended results.

Some specific challenges that can be faced in case study research include the potential for case studies to simply become descriptions of events that are open to the readers' interpretation and the potential for the process to become 'quasi-deductive'.[76] A stronger focus on theory can, however, help to overcome the first two of these potential weaknesses and improve the efficacy of case studies.[77] This can be achieved through 'systematic combining', as introduced earlier in this chapter, which provides a constructive 'non-linear, path-dependent process of combining efforts with the ultimate objective of matching theory and reality'.[78] This approach allows for the successive modification of the theoretical framework as new empirical findings emerge.

By working through the two-part process of the systematic combining model – 'matching' along with 'direction and redirection' – it was possible to weave together the emerging empirical findings and theoretical foundations for interpretation and analysis. 'Matching', firstly, was a constant process throughout the research study that involved identifying trends as they emerged in the fieldwork and ascertaining if these emerging findings were consistent with current theoretical interpretations. Where the empirical evidence and current theoretical frameworks did not match, reference was made back to a central conceptual model,[79] which could help to provide guidelines for understanding the empirical data.[80] This process helped to ensure that data was not forced to fit preconceived classifications but rather built from the findings of the data collection.[81]

The combination of data sources in the research process through 'direction and redirection', secondly – through including interviews, observations and documentation analysis – helped to ensure the case study was a deep dive into issues that took account of multiple perspectives.[82] This process was enhanced by simultaneously taking into account the different sources of evidence along with interpretation and analysis,[83] which can lead to uncovering new dimensions of the research problem. Observations can identify new questions on which further interviews can be based, which occurred in this case.

While research studies which focus on processes work within a limited time frame, the processes in the case organisation continued. This meant that any conclusions were bound by time constraints. The initial analytical framework needed to be broad enough to allow for emerging findings and to ensure there were no preconceptions and biases that might taint the way the data was viewed (e.g. loose and emergent), but also structured enough to provide guidelines for the research process (e.g. tight and pre-structured).[84]

The process of systematic combining involved integrating the theory with what was identified in practice to ensure there was a 'tight evolving' framework.[85] By continually referring to related literature during the research process, and by seeking new information from the literature as the results of the fieldwork process developed, it was possible to then link with existing theoretical and conceptual frameworks and direct the interpretation of the findings and identify if new territory is being uncovered.[86] A fundamental benefit of this approach for the researcher was that learning could take place 'in the interplay between search and discovery'.[87]

By 'bracketing' or linking discursive moments for analytical purposes, and by considering how sensemaking episodes are structured and what form they take, it also became possible to identify how the leaders constructed narratives.[88] Additionally, analysing metaphors assisted with identifying these patterns of self-construction.[89]

Focusing on metaphors

An analysis of metaphors in language and of the visual images constructed during the interview process enabled a rich insight into the core issues and challenges.

The use of metaphors, which is defined by the description of one thing in terms of something else, has been described as being a critical cognitive tool[90] and a 'fundamental scheme by which people conceptualise the world and their own activities'.[91] Where metaphors are analysed in context as integrated concepts[92] as 'applied linguistics',[93] and particularly in their cultural context,[94] they can provide rich insights into experiences.

Pictorial or visual metaphors have become the most studied forms of non-verbal metaphors,[95] and they have been specifically identified as providing a window into entrenched emotions and meanings. Metaphors have even been perceived as paradoxes, as they have been described as both creative and common.[96] Metaphors are a shifting dynamic phenomenon that can not only be a form of organisation and conceptualisation but also reveal deeper attitudes and values,[97] which was why there was a focus on analysing metaphors in this research. Analysing multimodal metaphors, as could be seen in the pictures created by the interviewees during the 'draw and talk' sessions, helped to reveal how the interviewees played with metaphoric possibilities[98] and how these metaphors often have a deeper emotional component that may be a strong influence on perspectives and actions.[99]

Analysis of conversation and discourse in this way is often used to study detailed processes,[100] as they work in real time. They can reveal the sensemaking process in detail, showing how sensemaking unfolds from one moment to the next, and it then becomes possible to see the often more hidden areas of team coordination and strategising.[101]

Weaving the data analysis process together

The data analysis process involved integrating a number of different techniques.

Firstly, an 'event history database'[102] was constructed from the interview data (general interviews plus an additional focused interview with a member of the senior leadership team who had been with the organisation from the beginning), archival data, journal notes and other documentation (internal documents, media reports, etc.).

An historical timeline was then constructed from the information gathered, which included external political events (such as government policies on refugees) along with internal organisational changes. This timeline was cross-checked by the GM and other senior leadership team members to ensure accuracy, and it therefore helped provide a context for the research by identifying external and internal factors impacting the organisation in general and the senior leadership team in particular over time.

Once the external context had been broadly identified, specific experiences or 'snapshots' of lived experience as observed in situ were then examined against this backdrop. The data from the drawings generated in the 'draw and talk' interviews was initially analysed in overview format by laying out all the drawings and related interview transcript data on a spreadsheet for comparison purposes and to identify potential patterns. Summaries of the interview data, drawings, documentation and observation notes from the research journal were included on the spreadsheet against the backdrop of the timeline to look for emergent patterns.

Coding the data in a computer program (NVivo) led to the identification of coarse general themes for initial analysis, including tensions at the organisation-level (political and socioeconomic context, organisation history, organisation values) and leadership-level (types of tensions, impact of tensions, strategies used to deal with tensions, paradoxical nature of tensions). The paradoxical tensions identified could be traced back to two different sensemaking perspectives related to variant responses to competing demands. Through an iterative process, one overarching integrated theme could be ascertained. Finally, a compilation narrative was constructed by weaving together the sensemaking strands. This emergent narrative is explored in detail in Chapter 4.

The methods chosen for the study provided rich insights into the leadership sensemaking dynamics and ensured a powerful platform for uncovering the emergent research findings.

REFLECTION AND ACTION QUESTIONS

Reflection

- Why was a case study methodology selected for studying for-purpose innovation leadership in an organisation?
- What research techniques were utilised in this case and why?
- How was it possible in this case research to get beyond more superficial interviews to ensure deeper insights?
- How was the data analysed, and how did this process help to enrich the outcomes?

Action

- For the study or work scenario you identified in the Reflection Questions from Chapter 2, consider how key information could be gathered. What methods do you think could be employed to ensure rich deep insights?
- Would a case study approach be appropriate for exploring this case? Why or why not?
- What techniques would you consider using to gain the best research insights?
- How could the data collected from your case study be effectively analysed?

Notes

1 Gioia and Chittipeddi, 1991, Gioia et al., 1994, Maitlis, 2005, Piekkari, Welch and Paavilainen, 2009, Weick, 1988, 1993
2 Yin 2014, p. 16
3 Yin, 2017
4 Ragin, 1992
5 Walker and Cohen, 1985
6 Ragin, 1992
7 Huberman and Miles, 1994
8 Pettigrew, 1990

9   Zalan and Lewis, 2004, p. 512
10 Riemer, 1977
11 Hayano, 1979, p. 100
12 Maitlis and Christianson, 2014
13 Balogun and Johnson, 2004
14 Gephart, Topal and Zhang, 2010
15 Donnellon, Gray and Bougon, 1986
16 Yin, 2003
17 Dubois and Gadde, 2002, p. 4554
18 Eisenhardt, 1991
19 Piekkari, Welch and Paavilainen, 2009
20 Dyer and Wilkins, 1991
21 Patton, 2002
22 Emmel, 2013, p. 142
23 Hennestad, 1999, Kalleberg, 1996
24 Finne, Levin and Nilssen, 1995
25 Welch et al., 2002
26 Stake, 2005
27 Stake, 2000, p. 441
28 Dubois and Araujo, 2004
29 Ragin, 1997
30 Van Maanen, 1988
31 Riemer, 1977
32 Hayano, 1979, p. 100
33 Van Maanen and Barley, 1984
34 Lincoln and Guba, 1985
35 Brannen, 1996
36 Smith, 2002, p. 384
37 Cooren, 2004, Liu and Maitlis, 2014
38 Langley, 1999, p. 162
39 Yin, 2003, p. 98
40 Siggelkow, 2007
41 Smith and Lewis, 2011
42 Besharov and Smith, 2014, Bowman, 2011, Dacin, Dacin and Tracey, 2011
43 Schaltegger and Wagner, 2011
44 Lervik, 2011, p. 231
45 Flick, 2009, Silverman, 1993
46 Gummesson, 1988, p. 76
47 Eisenhardt, 1989, p. 548
48 eg Balogun, Bartunek and Do, 2015
49 Atkinson and Hammersley, 1994, Emerson, Fretz and Shaw, 2001, Jorgensen, 2015, Spradley, 2016
50 Brown, Stacey and Nandhakumar, 2008, p. 1036
51 Höllerer, Jancsary and Grafström, 2018
52 Bell, Warren and Schroeder, 2014, Höllerer, Daudigeos and Jancsary, 2018
53 Campbell, 1975
54 Emmel, 2013
55 Leavy 2014, Parker, 2005
56 Leavy, 2014
57 Alvesson and Skoldberg, 2009
58 Backett-Milburn and McKie, 1999, Guillemin, 2004, Mitchell et al., 2011
59 Guillemin, 2004
60 Guillemin and Gillam, 2004

61 Barner, 2011, Kearney and Hyle, 2004, Vince and Warren, 2012
62 Alcadipani and Tonelli, 2014, Stiles, 2011, 2014
63 Han and Liang, 2015
64 Backett-Milburn and McKie, 1999, Guillemin, 2004, Kearney and Hyle, 2004, Mitchell et al., 2011
65 Kearney and Hyle, 2004
66 Mair and Kierans, 2007, Pink, 2008
67 Nossiter and Biberman, 1990
68 Alcadipani and Tonelli, 2014, Barner, 2011, Höllerer, Jancsary and Grafstron, 2018, Höykinpuro and Ropo, 2014
69 Brown, Stacey and Nandhakumar, 2008
70 Höllerer, Jancsary and Grafström, 2018
71 Bell, Warren and Schroeder, 2014, Höllerer, Daudigeos and Jancsary, 2018
72 as in Wright et al., 2012, p. 1461
73 Yin, 1994
74 Ragin, 1997, p. 30
75 Borghini, Carù and Cova, 2010
76 Easton, 1995, p. 379
77 Weick, 1979
78 Dubois and Gadde, 2002, p. 556
79 Richardson, 1972
80 Dubois and Gadde, 2002
81 Glaser, 1978
82 Yin, 1994
83 Denzin, 1978
84 Blumer, 1954, Bryman, 1995, Miles and Huberman, 1994
85 Dubois and Gadde, 2002, p. 558
86 Strauss and Corbin, 1990
87 Dubois and Gadde, 2002, p. 560
88 Holstein and Gubrium, 2000, Nyberg and Sveningsson, 2014
89 Johnson and Lackoff, 2003
90 Burke, 1945, Low, 2008
91 Gibbs, 2008, p. 3
92 Honeck, 1980
93 Cameron, 1999, p. 3
94 Yu, 2008
95 Carroll, 1994, Cupchik, 2003, Danto, 1993, Dent-Read and Szokolszky, 1993, Forceville, 2002, Kaplan, 1992, Maalej, 2001, Moulin, 2002
96 Gibbs, 2008
97 Cameron, 2008
98 Kennedy, 2008
99 Forceville, 2008
100 Maitlis and Christianson, 2014
101 Brown, 2000, Cooren, 2004, Hindmarsh and Pilnick, 2007, Liu and Maitlis, 2014, Maitlis and Christianson, 2014
102 Garud and Rappa, 1994, Karra, Tracey and Philipps, 2006

References

Alcadipani, R., & Tonelli, M. J. (2014). Imagining gender research: Violence, masculinity, and the shop floor. *Gender, Work & Organization, 21*(4), 321–339.

Alvesson, M., & Skoldberg, K. (2009). Positivism, social constructionism, critical realism: Three reference points in the philosophy of science. In K. Sköldberg &

M. Alvesson (Eds.), *Reflexive methodology: New vistas for qualitative research* (pp. 15–52). London: Sage.

Atkinson, P., & Hammersley, M. (1994). Ethnography and participant observation. In N. K. Denzin & Y. S. Lincoln (Eds.), *Handbook of qualitative research* (pp. 248–261). Thousand Oaks: Sage Publications.

Backett-Milburn, K., & McKie, L. (1999). A critical appraisal of the draw and write technique. *Health Education Research, 14*(3), 387–398.

Balogun, J., Bartunek, J. M., & Do, B. (2015). Senior managers' sensemaking and responses to strategic change. *Organization Science, 26*(4), 960–979.

Balogun, J., & Johnson, G. (2004). Organizational restructuring and middle manager sensemaking. *Academy of Management Journal, 47*(4), 523–549.

Barner, R. W. (2011). Applying visual metaphors to career transitions. *Journal of Career Development, 8*(1), 89–106.

Bell, E., Warren, S., & Schroeder, J. E. (Eds.) (2014). *The Routledge companion to visual organization*. New York: Routledge.

Besharov, M. L., & Smith, W. K. (2014). Multiple institutional logics in organizations: Explaining their varied nature and implications. *Academy of Management Review, 39*(3), 364–381.

Blumer, H. (1954). What is wrong with social theory? *American Sociological Review, 19*(1), 3–10.

Borghini, S., Carù, A., & Cova, B. (2010). Representing BtoB reality in case study research: Challenges and new opportunities. *Industrial Marketing Management, 39*(1), 16–24.

Bowman, W. (2011). Financial capacity and sustainability of ordinary nonprofits. *Nonprofit Management and Leadership, 22*(1), 37–51.

Brannen, M. Y. (1996). Ethnographic international management research. In B. J. Punnett & O. Shenkar (Eds.), *Handbook for international management research* (pp. 115–143). Cambridge: Blackwell.

Brown, A. D. (2000). Making sense of inquiry sensemaking. *Journal of Management Studies, 37*(1), 45–75.

Brown, A. D., Stacey, P., & Nandhakumar, J. (2008). Making sense of sensemaking narratives. *Human Relations, 61*(8), 1035–1062.

Bryman, A. (1995). *Quantity and quality in social research*. London: Unwin Hyman.

Burke, K. (1945). *A grammar of motives*. New York: Prentice-Hall.

Cameron, L. (1999). Operationalising 'metaphor' for applied linguistic research. In L. Cameron (Ed.), *Researching and applying metaphor* (pp. 3–28). Cambridge: Cambridge University Press.

Cameron, L. (2008). Metaphor and talk. In R. W. Gibbs Jr. (Ed.), *The Cambridge handbook of metaphor and thought* (pp. 197–211). Cambridge: Cambridge University Press.

Campbell, D. T. (1975). Degrees of freedom and the case study. *Comparative Political Studies, 8*(2), 178–193.

Carroll, N. (1994). Visual metaphor. In J. Hintikka (Ed.), *Aspects of metaphor* (pp. 189–218). Dordecht: Springer.

Cooren, F. (2004). The communicative achievement of collaborative minding: Analysis of boarding meeting excerpts. *Management Communication Quarterly, 17*(4), 517–551.

Cupchik, G. C. (2003). The 'interanimation' of worlds: Creative metaphors in art and design. *The Design Journal, 6*(2), 14–28.

Dacin, M. T., Dacin, P. A., & Tracey, P. (2011). Social entrepreneurship: A critique and future directions. *Organization Science, 22*(5), 1203–1213.

Danto, A. C. (1993). Metaphor and cognition. In F. R. Ankersmit & J. J. A. Mooij (Eds.), *Knowledge and language* (pp. 21–35). Dordrecht: Springer.

Dent-Read, C. H., & Szokolszky, A. (1993). Where do metaphors come from? *Metaphor and Symbol, 8*(3), 227–242.

Denzin, N. K. (1978). The logic of naturalistic inquiry. In N. K. Denzin (Ed.), *Sociological methods, a sourcebook* (pp. 54–73). New York: McGraw-Hill.

Donnellon, A., Gray, B., & Bougon, M. G. (1986). Communication, meaning, and organized action. *Administrative Science Quarterly, 31*(1), 43–55.

Dubois, A., & Araujo, L. (2004). Research methods in industrial marketing studies. In A. Waluszewski, D. Harrison, & H. Håkansson (Eds.), *Rethinking marketing: Developing a new understanding of markets* (pp. 207–227). Chichester: John Wiley and Sons Ltd.

Dubois, A., & Gadde, L. E. (2002). Systematic combining: An abductive approach to case research. *Journal of Business Research, 55*(7), 553–560.

Dyer, W. G., & Wilkins, A. L. (1991). Better stories, not better constructs, to generate better theory: A rejoinder to Eisenhardt. *Academy of Management Review, 16*(3), 613–619.

Easton, G. (1995). Case research as a methodology for industrial networks: A realist apologia. *Proceedings from the 11th IMP Conference*, Manchester Federal School of Business and Management, Manchester, pp. 368–391.

Eisenhardt, K. M. (1989). Building theories from case study research. *Academy of Management Review, 14*(4), 532–550.

Eisenhardt, K. M. (1991). Better stories and better constructs: The case for rigor and comparative logic. *Academy of Management Review, 16*(3), 620–627.

Emerson, R. M., Fretz, R. I., & Shaw, L. L. (2001). Participant observation and fieldnotes. In L. H. Lofland, S. Delamont, A. Coffey, P. Atkinson, & J. Lofland (Eds.), *Handbook of ethnography* (pp. 352–368). Thousand Oaks: Sage.

Emmel, N. (2013). *Sampling and choosing cases in qualitative research: A realist approach*. London: Sage.

Finne, H., Levin, M., & Nilssen, T. (1995). Trailing research: A model for useful program evaluation. *Evaluation, 1*(1), 11–31.

Flick, U. (2009). *An introduction to qualitative research*. Thousand Oaks: Sage.

Forceville, C. (2002). The identification of target and source in pictorial metaphors. *Journal of Pragmatics, 34*(1), 1–14.

Forceville, C. (2008). Metaphor in pictures and multimodal representations. In R. W. Gibbs, *The Cambridge handbook of metaphor and thought* (pp. 462–482).

Garud, R., & Rappa, M. A. (1994). A socio-cognitive model of technology evolution: The case of cochlear implants. *Organization Science, 5*(3), 344–362.

Gephart, R. P., Topal, C., & Zhang, Z. (2010). Future-oriented sensemaking: Temporalities and institutional legitimation. In S. Maitlis & T. Hernes (Eds.), *Process, sensemaking, and organizing* (pp. 275–312). Oxford: Oxford University Press.

Gibbs Jr, R. W. (Ed.) (2008). *The Cambridge handbook of metaphor and thought*. Cambridge: Cambridge University Press.

Gioia, D., & Chittipeddi, K. (1991). Sensemaking and sensegiving in strategic change initiation. *Strategic Management Journal, 12*(6), 433–448.

Gioia, D. A., Thomas, J. B., Clark, S. M., & Chittipeddi, K. (1994). Symbolism and strategic change in academia: The dynamics of sensemaking and influence. *Organization Science, 5*(3), 363–383.

Glaser, B. G. (1978). *Theoretical sensibility*. Mill Valley: Sociology Press.

Guillemin, M. (2004). Understanding illness: Using drawings as a research method. *Qualitative Health Research, 14*(2), 272–289.

Guillemin, M., & Gillam, L. (2004). Ethics, reflexivity, and "ethically important moments" in research. *Qualitative Inquiry, 10*(2), 261–280.

Gummesson, E. (1988). *Qualitative methods in management research*. Thousand Oaks: Sage Publications.

Han, J., & Liang, N. (2015). In their own eyes and voices: The value of an executive MBA program according to participants. *Journal of Management Education, 39*(6), 741–773.

Hayano, D. M. (1979). Auto-ethnography. *Human Organization, 38*(1), 99–104.

Hennestad, B. W. (1999). Kritiske valg I forskning på organisasjonsendringer [Critical choices in research on organizational change]. In K. Friedman & J. Olaisen (Eds.), *Underveis til fremtiden: kunnskapsledelse i teori og prakis [On the way to the future: knowledge management in theory and practice* (pp. 71–89)]. Oslo: Fagbokforlaget.

Hindmarsh, J., & Pilnick, A. (2007). Knowing bodies at work: Embodiment and ephemeral teamwork in anaesthesia. *Organization Studies, 28*(9), 1395–1416.

Höllerer, M. A., Daudigeos, T., & Jancsary, D. (2018). Multimodality, meaning, and institutions: Editorial. *Research in the Sociology or Organizations, 54A*, 1–24.

Höllerer, M. A., Jancsary, D., & Grafström, M. (2018). A picture is worth a thousand words: Multimodal sensemaking of the global financial crisis. *Organization Studies, 39*(5–6), 617–644.

Holstein, J., & Gubrium, J. F. (2000). *The self we live by: Narrative identity in a postmodern world*. Oxford: Oxford University Press.

Honeck, R. P. (1980). Historical notes on figurative. In R. P. Honeck & R. R. Hoffman (Eds.), *Cognition and figurative language* (p. 25). Abingdon: Routledge.

Höykinpuro, R., & Ropo, A. (2014). Visual narratives on organizational space. *Journal of Organizational Change Management, 27*(5), 780–792.

Huberman, A. M., & Miles, M. B. (1994). Data management and analysis methods. In N. K. Denzin & Y. S. Lincoln (Eds.), *Handbook of qualitative research* (pp. 428–444). Thousand Oaks: Sage.

Johnson, M., & Lakoff, G. (2003). *Metaphors we live by*. Chicago and London: University of Chicago Press.

Jorgensen, D. L. (2015). Participant observation. In R. A Scott, R. H. Scott, S. M. Kosslyn, & M. C. Buchmann (Eds.), *Emerging trends in the social and behavioral sciences: An interdisciplinary, searchable, and linkable resource* (pp. 1–15). Brisbane: John Wiley and Sons.

Kalleberg, R. (1996). Forord: feltmetodikk, forskningsopplegg og vitenskapsteori' [Foreword: field study methodology research design and the theory of science]. In M. Hammersley & P. Atkinson (Eds.), *Feltmetodikk [Field study methodology* (pp. 5–28)]. Oslo: ad Notam.

Kaplan, S. J. (1992). A conceptual analysis of form and content in visual metaphors. *Communication, 13*, 197–209.

Karra, N., Tracey, P., & Phillips, N. (2006). Altruism and agency in the family firm: Exploring the role of family, kinship, and ethnicity. *Entrepreneurship Theory and Practice, 30*(6), 861–877.

Kearney, K. S., & Hyle, A. E. (2004). Drawing out emotions: The use of participant-produced drawings in qualitative inquiry. *Qualitative Research, 4*(3), 361–382.

Kennedy, J. M. (2008). Metaphor and art. In R. W. Gibbs (Ed.), *The Cambridge handbook of metaphor and thought* (pp. 447–461). Cambridge: Cambridge University Press.

Langley, A. (1999). Strategies for theorizing from process data. *Academy of Management Review, 24*(4), 691–710.

Leavy, P. (2014). *The Oxford handbook of qualitative research.* Oxford: Oxford University Press.

Lervik, M. E. (2011). The single MNC as a research site. In R. Piekkari & C. Welch (Eds.), *Rethinking the case study in international business and management research* (pp. 229–250). Cheltenham: Edward Elgar.

Lincoln, Y. S., & Guba, E. G. (1985). *Naturalistic inquiry.* Beverly Hills: Sage Publications.

Liu, F., & Maitlis, S. (2014). Emotional dynamics and strategizing processes: A study of strategic conversations in top team meetings. *Journal of Management Studies, 51*(2), 202–234.

Low, G. (2008). Metaphor and education. In Gibbs, R. W. *The Cambridge handbook of metaphor and thought.* Cambridge: Cambridge University Press.

Maalej, Z. (2001). Processing pictorial metaphor in advertising: A cross-cultural perspective. *Academic Research, 1*(1), 19–42.

Mair, M., & Kierans, C. (2007). Descriptions as data: Developing techniques to elicit descriptive materials in social research. *Visual Studies, 22*(2), 120–136.

Maitlis, S. (2005). The social processes of organizational sensemaking. *Academy of Management Journal, 48*(1), 21–49.

Maitlis, S., & Christianson, M. (2014). Sensemaking in organizations: Taking stock and moving forward. *Academy of Management Annals, 8*(1), 57–125.

Miles, M. B., & Huberman, A. M. (1994). *Qualitative data analysis: An expanded sourcebook.* Thousand Oaks: Sage.

Mitchell, M., Theron, L., Stuart, J., Smith, A., & Campbell, Z. (2011). Drawings as a research method. In L. Theron, M. Mitchell, A. Smith, & J. Stuart (Eds.), *Picturing research, drawing as visual methodology* (pp. 19–36). Rotterdam: Sense Publishers.

Moulin, A. (2002). *Metaphor and visual imagery in advertising.* [Unpublished MA thesis - University of Ghent, Department. of Germanic languages, Belgium].

Nossiter, V., & Biberman, G. (1990). Projective drawings and metaphor: Analysis of organisational culture. *Journal of Managerial Psychology, 5*(3), 13–16.

Nyberg, D., & Sveningsson, S. (2014). Paradoxes of authentic leadership: Leader identity struggles. *Leadership, 10*(4), 437–455.

Parker, I. (2005). *Qualitative psychology: Introducing radical research.* Oxford: Open University Press.

Patton, M. Q. (2002). Designing qualitative studies. *Qualitative Research and Evaluation Methods, 3*, 230–246.

Pettigrew, A. M. (1990). Longitudinal field research on change: Theory and practice. *Organization Science, 1*(3), 267–292.

Piekkari, R., Welch, C., & Paavilainen, E. (2009). The case study as disciplinary convention: Evidence from international business. *Organizational Research Methods, 12*(3), 567–589.

Pink, S. (2008). Mobilising visual ethnography: Making routes, making place and making images. *Forum Qualitative Sozialforschung (Forum: Qualitative Social Research)*, 9(3). Art. 36.

Ragin, C. C. (1992). Casing and the process of social inquiry. In C. C. Ragin & H. S. Becker (Eds.), *What is a case? Exploring the foundations of social inquiry* (pp. 217–222). New York: Cambridge University Press.

Ragin, C. C. (1997). Turning the tables: How case-oriented research challenges variable-oriented research. *Comparative Social Research, 16*(1), 27–42.

Richardson, G. B. (1972). The organisation of industry. *Economic Journal, 82*(327), 883–896.

Riemer, J. W. (1977). Varieties of opportunistic research. *Urban Life, 5*(4), 467–477.

Schaltegger, S., & Wagner, M. (2011). Sustainable entrepreneurship and sustainability innovation: Categories and interactions. *Business Strategy and the Environment, 20*(4), 222–237.

Siggelkow, N. (2007). Persuasion with case studies. *Academy of Management Journal, 50*(1), 20–24.

Silverman, D. (1993). *Beginning research: Interpreting qualitative data. Methods for analysing talk, text and interaction.* London: Sage Publications.

Smith, A. D. (2002). From process data to publication: A personal sensemaking. *Journal of Management Inquiry, 11*(4), 383–406.

Smith, W. K., & Lewis, M. W. (2011). Toward a theory of paradox: A dynamic equilibrium model of organizing. Academy of Management Review, 36(2), 381–403.

Spradley, J. P. (2016). *Participant observation.* Illinois: Waveland Press.

Stake, R. (2005). Qualitative case studies. In N. K. Denzin & Y. S. Lincoln (Eds.), *The Sage handbook of qualitative research* (pp. 448–459). Thousand Oaks: Sage Publications.

Stake, R. E. (2000). Case studies. In N. Denzin & Y. Lincoln (Eds.), *Handbook of qualitative research* (pp. 435–454). Thousand Oaks: Sage Publications.

Stiles, D. R. (2011). Disorganization, disidentification and ideological fragmentation: Verbal and pictorial evidence from a British business school. *Culture and Organization, 17*(1), 5–30.

Stiles, D. R. (2014). Drawing as a method of organizational analysis. In *The Routledge companion to visual organization* (pp. 227–258). Abingdon: Routledge.

Strauss, A., & Corbin, J. (1990). *Basics of qualitative research.* Thousand Oaks: Sage.

Van Maanen, J. (1988). *Tales of the field.* Chicago: University of Chicago Press.

Van Maanen, J., & Barley, S. R. (1984). Occupational communities: Culture and control in organizations. *Research in Organizational Behaviour, 6*, 287–365.

Vince, R., & Warren, S. (2012). Participatory visual methods 16. In G. Symon & C. Cassell (Eds.), *Qualitative organizational research: Core methods and current challenges* (p. 275). London: Sage.

Walker, H. A., & Cohen, B. P. (1985). Scope statements: Imperatives for evaluating theory. *American Sociological Review, 50*(3), 288–301.

Weick, K. E. (1979). *The social psychology of organizing* (2nd ed.). New York: McGraw-Hill.

Weick, K. E. (1988). Enacted sensemaking in crisis situations. *Journal of Management Studies*, *25*(4), 305–317.

Weick, K. E. (1993). The collapse of sensemaking in organizations: The Mann Gulch disaster. *Administrative Science Quarterly*, *38*(4), 628–652.

Welch, C., Marschan-Piekkari, R., Penttinen, H., & Tahvanainen, M. (2002). Corporate elites as informants in qualitative international business research. *International Business Review*, *11*(5), 611–628.

Wright, C., Nyberg, D., & Grant, D. (2012). Hippies on the third floor: Climate change, narrative identity and the micro-politics of corporate environmentalism. *Organization Studies*, *33*(11), 1451–1475.

Yin, R. K. (1994). *Case study research: Design and methods* (2nd ed.). London: Sage.

Yin, R. K. (2003). *Case study research: Design and methods* (3rd ed.). Thousand Oaks: Sage.

Yin, R. K. (2014). *Case study research: Design and methods* (5th ed.). Thousand Oaks: Sage.

Yin, R. K. (2017). *Case study research and applications: Design and methods*. Thousand Oaks: Sage.

Yu, N. (2008). Metaphor from body and culture. In R. W. Gibbs (Ed.), *The Cambridge handbook of metaphor and thought* (pp. 247–261). Cambridge: Cambridge University Press.

Zalan, T., & Lewis, G. (2004). Writing about methods in qualitative research: Towards a more transparent approach. In R. Marschan-Piekkari & C. Welch (Eds.), *Handbook of qualitative research methods for international business* (pp. 507–528). Cheltenham: Edward Elgar.

4 What the research revealed

The unique innovation findings

OVERVIEW

The rigorous data collection process yielded some fascinating results. This chapter reveals the key insights.

The first half of the chapter discusses the relevant ***background factors that led to tensions***, which were uncovered early in the research process. Firstly, there were some clear insights into the challenges emerging from the complex rapid-change context and the impact on the case organisation. As the organisation grew rapidly in response to perceived needs, there were some clear changes in identity – including a shift from a simple not-for-profit status to include a social enterprise arm and a transition from more of a grass roots 'community movement' to a more 'corporatised' structure. Additionally, the impact of a number of external forces was clear – particularly, the economic and political culture, rapidly changing government policies and the inevitable social shift in the migrant and refugee (M&R) experience and status as they transitioned from government dependence to integration into local communities.

The second half of the chapter provides ***insights into how innovation was navigated over time***. It illuminates the unique sensemaking actions and reactions that were observed during the research process. When observing the senior leadership team dynamics, it soon became clear that initially the focus for the leaders was on coping with and surviving the crisis that had emerged from a period of rapid innovation and growth (scaling up). As staff experienced the chaos and isolation from a lack of clarity and alignment, perhaps inevitably innovation alignment challenges became amplified. The turning point came with the engagement of a new senior leader, who provided an alternative approach to the established 'innovative social entrepreneur' style. As

DOI: 10.4324/9781003426691-4

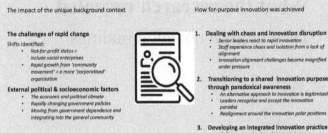

Figure 4.1 Revealing the key findings

the two polar perspectives became accepted and legitimised as important complementary positions, the staff were able to realign around these validated polar stances. This indicates the development of collective paradoxical cognition.

A workable dynamic balance was eventually reached when an integrated innovation practice was established, which involved rallying around a shared integrated story that reaffirmed the core mission and purpose (Figure 4.1).

Identifying the core challenge area

Case study research is a little like a police investigation. There will be specific 'clues' or data points. Interviews will reveal different perspectives and stories on key incidents, and the evidence must be identified and scrutinised in great detail to look for key patterns and themes.

An important objective of the research program was to study the micro-foundations of leadership in innovation contexts to identify useful strategic and practical insights for senior leaders. The research program evolved as an in-depth study into how senior leaders experience and respond to competing demands in the context of innovation, according to the research question introduced earlier: *How do leaders experience and respond to competing innovation demands in for-purpose-driven innovation?*

The case study approach made it possible to observe the dynamics between senior leaders in context, particularly noting how individuals with different cognitive frames and mindsets came together to negotiate collaborative alignment in response to competing innovation demands. Early observations of the senior leadership team in the case organisation confirmed the importance of considering different levels of analysis. As identified in the last chapter, two specific areas of focus were the senior leadership team as a standard operational unit (including the Chief Executive Officer (CEO), Chief Operating Officer (COO) and their direct reports, the directors), along with the powerful core senior leadership duo of the CEO and COO embedded within the team. The senior leadership team was an intact pre-existing group and as the members were part of the executive team and shared common experiences, it made most sense to focus on this group.[1]

Background to the case organisation

The 'Social Support Organisation' (SSO) studied initially started as a 'grassroots movement' led by a passionate individual with a clear social purpose in response to the critical needs experienced by people seeking asylum.

The enterprise was established in response to an immediate crisis, and in the 15 years following, it constantly rapidly adapted and expanded according to the external environmental challenges and the changing needs of M&Rs. The mandate had always been to 'turn no one in need away', and as a result, the organisation adapted rapidly over the years. Both the shift from a clear social purpose towards a more commercial model and the rapid growth of the enterprise led to inherent tensions within the organisation that impacted the senior leadership team strategies and decisions.

The CEO was proud of being innovative, and innovation was included in the organisation vision as a core value. More than 30 innovative programs had been designed to address the immediate and ongoing needs of new arrivals in the country. Yet it appeared that the innovation and growth had been too fast. As a result, the enterprise had experienced an ongoing sense of crisis with a great deal of uncertainty about its future, despite having grown to become a large and apparently well-established organisation. Table 4.1 summarises the important demographic features of the organisation.

The organisation was vulnerable to a number of significant factors that had a major impact on the senior leaders: *rapid change* – including a shift in not-for-profit status to social enterprise and rapid growth in size, along with the impact of significant external *political and socioeconomic factors*. The enterprise was being stretched to reconsider its values base, in terms of values focus, experiencing a shift from a clear not-for-profit status to include social enterprises to better support becoming more financially sustainable. Senior leaders were also being overextended in trying to accommodate the different needs and requirements of these shifts.

This next section outlines some of these key factors impacting the organisation.

Table 4.1 Summary demographic details of SSO at the time of study

Demographics	Details
Description of organisation	Large provider of aid, legal, material, educational and health services to vulnerable migrants and people seeking asylum
Structure	An independent, community-led organisation (runs on donations – does not receive government funding)
Senior management team roles	Senior management team roles include: • CEO • COO • Humanitarian services (food bank, food truck, etc.) • Advocacy and campaigns (legal) • People and culture (people management) • Shared business services (operations, IT, facilities) • Innovation Hub (education, employment, mentoring, social and community development, youth, women, new social enterprises) • Social enterprises (business incubation and business support) • Fundraising and marketing
Programs offered	A large number of holistic programs that 'protect members from persecution and destitution, support well-being and dignity, and empower people to advance their own future', including services in the following areas: • Legal • Health • Casework • Food and material support • Employment and training • English language classes • Entrepreneurs program • Social and community development • Community meals The organisation incorporated two innovative new social enterprise services designed to give people seeking asylum work experience opportunities: • Catering business • Cleaning business

Rapid change

Shift from not-for-profit status to include social enterprises

The organisation had been deliberate in its mission to retain a not-for-profit status to be able to act 'without fear or favour', yet it was constantly under pressure to fundraise for donations. To address this issue, SSO established services designed to make it more commercially sustainable, in particular social enterprises, which potentially impacted its not-for-profit purpose and status.

There was a clear tension for the organisation leadership between the need to balance the focus on retaining a clear purpose while, on the other hand, trying to remain financially viable. These related tensions were exacerbated over time as the organisation continued to grow, and the need for more resources became more critical. The core tension was most apparent in a competition for resources and disagreements about how funding should be used. The rapid growth of the organisation also resulted in challenges in determining strategic focus.

Rapid growth from 'community movement' to a more 'corporatised' organisation

As the enterprise was initially highly agile and responsive to member needs, SSO grew rapidly. This adaptive and innovative approach led to the rapid transition of the organisation from a small founder-led 'community movement' to a large entity requiring more of a 'professional' or 'corporate' structure.

Immediately prior to the start of the research period, the organisation had been through a particularly rapid period of innovation and growth in an attempt to deal with increasing member needs (up to 2,000 per year) due to changing government policies. This rapid growth prompted a move to a new property much larger than the previous premises and a corresponding dramatic increase in the number of staff (up to 120) and volunteers (up to 1,000), which had, in turn, led to significant strategic dissent at the senior leadership level.

External political and socioeconomic factors

The volatile political, economic and sociological climate also had a significant impact on the SSO's work and affected their and strategic purpose. The organisation was initially established to provide immediate material support (food, clothing, etc) for vulnerable people in response to a crisis triggered by adverse political events.

As the awareness of the ongoing needs of these people grew, the enterprise took on additional functions to help to support a shift from simply 'surviving' to 'thriving' (terms often used by organisation members to describe both the historical development of the services offered by the organisation and the distinct current parallel streams of services offered).

The construction of the historical overview revealed significant external political and socioeconomic factors and their impact on internal development leading up to the period of research. The analysis of factors that had led to the critical crisis period immediately prior to the research was important, as these

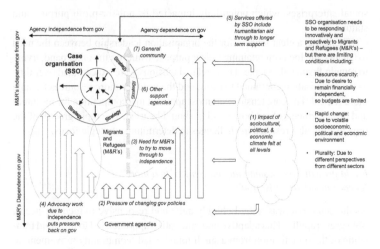

Figure 4.2 Context of SSO work, showing external factors impacting the organisation

factors had put a significant amount of stress on the organisation and the leaders and had culminated in the departure of a number of senior executives and other staff along with attracting high-profile negative media attention.

As a highly responsive organisation established to meet the needs of a vulnerable population, it was expected that a number of external factors would have a significant impact on the way the organisation functioned and on strategic decisions made by the senior leadership team.

Figure 4.2 reveals some significant external pressures and related needs. The diagram was designed to show the deep impact of a range of external factors that put pressure on the organisation, particularly the political and economic climate and associated government policies.

The external pressures include:

1   the direct and indirect impact of the economic and political climate on vulnerable M&Rs
2   the specific pressures placed on people M&Rs by rapidly changing government policies
3   the need for M&Rs to shift away from government dependence and integrate into the general community.

The diagram also reveals the role of the case organisation SSO in assisting with this transition for people seeking asylum into the community through:
4   advocating on M&R issues to the government (which was possible due to the organisation's independence from the government by not receiving federal government funding, in contrast to other similar agencies),

offering services including humanitarian services for new arrivals (providing food, material needs, housing, health care, legal services) and additional services for more settled clients (education, employment training, employment opportunities and community integration through leisure activities).

Further segments of the diagram show additional stakeholders involved, including:
5 the work done with other agencies in the sector (e.g. through networks, working groups and shared advocacy)
6 the work done with the general community (e.g. through fundraising, community engagement activities, etc.).

This figure also shows the points of contact with each external stakeholder group. These points of contact reveal the strategic need to continue to expand and remain flexible to best meet these needs, along with the counteractive consolidation force required to ensure there are systems and structures in place that can support growth. These points of contact have shaped the foundation of the seven streams of the organisation, led by each of the seven directors in the senior leadership team, as shown in Figure 4.3. The division between the 'Internal Facing' and 'External Facing' streams was found to be particularly significant in the different sensemaking perspectives identified. The rapid transitions between the different positions identified in this diagram helped to reveal the potential for dynamic tensions.

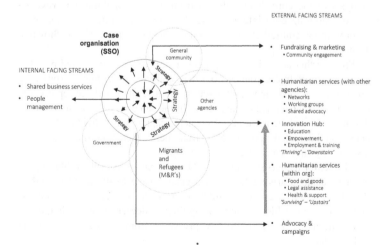

Figure 4.3 SSO's seven internal and external facing streams

The senior leadership team of seven directors plus the COO and CEO met weekly for two hours to discuss projects and make strategic decisions. At the time of the research, they were working on the business plans for the catering and cleaning businesses. The director team was concerned that the group had not yet had enough time to make strategic decisions around this issue, and it had become a source of tension within the group.

How innovation alignment was achieved

There were a number of different findings from the research as outcomes of the 'investigative police work', particularly from triangulating the information collected from the observations, interviews and drawings generated through the 'draw and talk' technique and particularly considering the extensive metaphors participants referred to in their interviews. Most significantly, a number of paradoxical tensions emerged – 16 in total. These tensions were found to be related to two core sensemaking orientations connected to significant competing demands.

These two core orientations were identified at the leadership level and were potentially cascading to other levels of the organisation – or perhaps the leaders were reflecting the core perspectives of employees at other levels. Regardless, the tensions could then be mapped back to the following two key sensemaking perspectives that appeared to align with the different CEO and COO narratives. These narratives were related to (1) a desire to focus on developing strategic roles and relationships (aligning to the CEO perspective) and (2) a desire to focus on developing strategic systems and structures (aligning to the COO perspective). Overall, an analysis of the core themes drawn from the sensemaking data revealed one overarching core integrated need for aligned strategic development incorporating contradictory and complementary elements, as shown in Table 4.2.

From further analysis, a compilation narrative was constructed based on the collation of freeze frames from data collected over time. Through this process, it was possible to pull together a rich dramatic collage representing the senior leadership team experience. In the same way that a storyboard is designed to combine a variety of concepts captured in individual frames to convey an integrated story, the clues from these different perspectives helped discern a dynamic emerging core narrative.

The senior leadership team at SSO was found to be vulnerable to paradoxical tensions arising from rapid change (due to the rapid growth of the organisation), resource limitations (due to a reliance on donations and volunteers, which created a significant degree of unpredictability) and plurality (leading to diverse pressures from external and internal stakeholders).

Table 4.2 Summary of sensemaking orientations identified in the data

Position	Past state	Current state	Desired future state	Personal journey	How to reach desired future state	Key themes	Sensemaking perspectives	Core integrated need
	Survival 'Trying to keep heads above water' Chaos & siloes	**Transitioning** 'At a crossroads - stepping up & filling gaps' Moving forward	**Thriving** 'Harmony & running like clockwork' Connectedness, & alignment	**Dealing with instability** 'Navigating minefields'	**Importance of strategic focus** 'Exercise of progression' Consistency, accountability, courage			**The need for aligned strategic development incorporating contradictory & complementary paradoxical concepts**
Aligned with CEO	'Lost'	'Happy'	'More "linked"'	Aiming for finish line with others	'Learn from each other'	Connection	**Focus on the need to develop strategic roles & relationships:** Desired to Transition from isolated to connected & aligned	
	'Working in siloes'	'Some connections, but not all - & exhausted'	'Working together more effectively, more accountable'	'Challenge', 'emotional'	'Collective responsibility', 'Sharing'	Accountability		
	New to organisation	'Siloes', 'satellites', 'cliques'	'Interconnected', 'equal'	New to organisation	'Mutual accountability', 'More courageous conversations'	Openness		
	'Not enough support'	'More support'	'Happy'		'Consistent communication'	Support		
	'Contained chaos', 'grown from ashes'	'Void', 'at a crossroads'	'Harmony', 'same direction'	'Ups & downs, plateau'		Harmony		
	'Artificial harmony', 'CEO omnipresent'	'Disparity', 'unconscious resistance'	'Yin & yang'	'Ultimately optimistic'	'Exercise of progress not perfection'	Synergy		
	'Gap', 'Wall Straddling', 'Some personal connections'	'Now more transparent', 'working better'	'All together inside'	'Ups & downs', 'doors & windows' (more open)	'Focus on horizon' More 'trust on organisation wide business decisions'	Trust		
						Transparency		
		'Movie with different scripts'		'Ups and downs', 'minefields'		Alignment		
Aligned with COO	Need for strategic organisation	More organised but under dominant CEO	'Take a big picture view'		'Strategic management'	Strategic view	**Focus on the need to develop strategic systems & structures:** Desired to Transition from chaotic to efficient & controlled	
	'Trying to keep heads above water'	'Moving forward'	Becoming more profitable		'More professional' 'Corporate' 'Less Grassroots'	Profitable		
	'Jumping holes'	'Stepping up'	'Running like clockwork'		'Strategic direction'	Professional		
	'Gaps'	'Filling the gaps'	'Solid base to launch from'		'Filling in the gaps'	Solid structure		
	'Drowning in the day-to-day'	'Too much reliance on CEO'	'Team in lock & step in sync around models'	Hopeful	'Discipline' 'Transparency' 'Change Management'	Discipline		
						Clear systems		

The analysis of the case study data revealed distinctly evolving sensemaking orientations within the senior leadership team related to how the members responded to the organisation's growing structure in reaction to the changing demands. The following compilation narrative was constructed from the observed sensemaking episodes to demonstrate the historical development of the predominant sensemaking orientations and shifting allegiances over three approximate time periods of the research, showing how collective alignment was negotiated in practice.

The nature of the evolving episodic story as a process demonstrates how these paradoxical tensions can accumulate over time and ripple and cascade throughout the organisation, leading to a compounding impact on people in different areas and at different levels of the organisation. The three phases were identified in the transition of allegiance as part of the gradual shift towards senior leadership team alignment and strategic focus for more effective high-impact innovation and growth:

1 *Dealing with chaos and innovation disruption*
2 *Transitioning to a shared innovation purpose through paradoxical awareness*
3 *Developing an integrated innovation practice*

Dealing with chaos and innovation disruption

The beginning of the research period was characterised by chaos due to the disruption from rapid innovation and growth.

Ironically, while the signature innovative approach had been essential for addressing critical issues and meeting core member needs, the pace of change had also disrupted the organisation and created new challenges in itself. On the one hand, the organisation had been highly innovative, agile and adaptive in alignment with the entrepreneurial CEO's approach and in response to the rapidly changing needs. On the other hand, there was growing discontent and dissent around the disruptions from this innovation.

Divergent strategic perspectives within the senior leadership team on how to deal with increasing pressure from the government and related member needs led to differing expectations. This, in turn, generated significant tensions, which eventually resulted in insurmountable conflict within the team and a major crisis for the organisation.

Senior leaders react to rapid innovation

Before the official research period began, there had been clear established roles with everyone reporting to the CEO, who represented the responsive, passionate, innovative sensemaking orientation he had established and maintained as the entrepreneurial founder. Leading up to the crisis in the organisation, although there had been formal reporting lines from all directors in the senior leadership team to the CEO according to the organisation chart, most senior leadership team members had developed different understandings of the core purpose and how it could be achieved, which led to the dissent and disillusionment.

As there was no alternative position officially represented at the top executive level, anyone who did not agree with the CEO's position and started to question the validity of alternative ways of achieving the mission was seen to be in 'opposition' to the CEO and the organisation and was identified as 'betraying' the core purpose and values of the organisation. As the CEO said soon after this period, 'You're trying to stay focused on mission and purpose and what you're there for, and then others try to do the very opposite'.

A combative relationship developed between the CEO, who as the founder of the organisation believed these views reflected the mission and purpose of the organisation, and the dissenting directors in the team, who had expressed that the lack of adequate systems and structures was stunting the organisation's ability to achieve its mission.

Staff experience chaos and isolation from a lack of alignment

The result was a 'chaotic' or misaligned culture that led to unresolvable tensions, which ultimately surfaced as a major organisation crisis with six of the seven directors resigning along with dozens of other staff. At this time one of the departing directors also lodged a successful legal claim for work induced stress and anxiety. This indicated a disconnection from the CEO and the established values and vision.

A number of the senior leadership team reported feeling 'lonely', 'lost' and 'isolated' and described the team as working in 'silos', 'satellites' and 'cliques', with 'some connection but not all'. Other terms used to describe how the directors felt about the impact on the way the organisation was running at the time indicated there were significant shortcomings in organisation effectiveness, such as 'jumping holes', 'wall straddling' and dealing with 'gaps'. The result was that the senior leadership team members felt like they were just 'drowning in the day-to-day', 'trying to keep their heads above water' and constantly navigating 'minefields'. The directors who had remained following the crisis described a type of 'post-traumatic stress' and appeared to be highly cautious and reserved about opening up too much and becoming vulnerable. There was a polite working relationship – what the COO described as an 'artificial harmony' – but the CEO's strong approach had appeared to alienate a number of people who had an opposing viewpoint. These perspectives became particularly obvious from the pictures the leaders drew to describe how they felt in the draw and talk sessions.

The growing distance between the CEO and members of the senior leadership team, which became inevitable as more people were recruited into the team, meant that the 'charismatic' influence had less impact. These new team members did not have a history with the strong organisation story that had been established by the CEO at the beginning and which had been built on and embellished over time. During this stage, the meeting agendas were formal and segmented, and the directors reported having to compete for resources. As one director expressed at the time, there was the feeling they were 'at a crossroads' and that there would be a 'void' unless the 'ups and downs' were adequately dealt with and some sort of strategic alignment and harmony could be reached in order for the senior leadership team and the organisation to start 'running like clockwork'. The visual representations of these metaphorical perspectives were particularly striking.

A member of the senior leadership team who had been promoted to fill one of the director positions left vacant following the crisis had been with the organisation since its inception and had maintained a close personal relationship with the CEO through this time. This director reflected on how the crisis 'was like a plague that went through the (organisation), it was like a ground attack, and then all the initial bullying (from the departing directors), and then it was like this whole kind of time in the trenches, just trying to manage'.

Another employee anonymously reported to the media at the time that the board supported the director and maintained a focus on the mission of the organisation, illuminating that 'front of the board's mind is always a desperate desire to help (clients, which) drives every decision, and sometimes the HR issues become secondary, or lost, because helping (clients) is the focus'.

Innovation alignment challenges become magnified under pressure

A director who had been with the organisation from the early days explained how the strong vision of the charismatic entrepreneurial leader had initially 'got us through the tough times' of the rapid growth in the early years as there was a shared passion with 'colleagues, we had our friends around us'. Then, as this director had explained, the crisis had 'changed the way in which we all interact with each other… it's definitely changed me'.

The CEO interpreted the core underlying challenges of this time as follows:

> *People's own power hunger and ego and jealousy and God knows what else took hold, and trust broke down… How would we never get to a place again where people are allowed to be so destructive and people are allowed to be so harmful and people are allowed to act in ways that work in complete betrayal of our values and our culture?... That's where we're more vulnerable – we have an idea that there's a shared altruism, or a shared compassion, a shared all-encompassing values that people are going honour and stay true to, and I think we expect that, and I think that's*

where we're more vulnerable, wherein corporates – corporates are used to predatory dog-eat-dog. Charities were not used to that, and we rely a lot on informal trust and informal agreement and informal integrity.

When the new COO position was set up, the CEO had already established a strong apparently unyielding position on the way the organisation should be run. Despite the crisis with the departure of the directors, the CEO had maintained a stance as an omnipresent leader, and the apparent choice had been to either align with the CEO or leave.

The transition to senior leadership team alignment was characterised by the arrival of the new COO and the consolidation of the new director team in response to the crisis. An intriguing general finding of the research was that the organisation itself appeared to mirror a common experience of the vulnerable people they were working with: there was a constant sense of crisis and, over time, there was a clear struggle to embrace the opposing orientation, including the focus from simply 'surviving' to go on to become a 'thriving' organisation.

This led to the shift from the purely 'responsive, innovative, passionate' orientation of the founding CEO to also incorporate the 'efficiency, control, consolidation' orientation that the COO introduced, with the recognition that both were equally important.

Transitioning to a shared innovation purpose through paradoxical awareness

There were still clear tensions in the senior leadership team when the new COO arrived. Although the tensions were not overt in the team meetings, it was possible to detect hypersensitivity in the way the senior leadership team communicated with each other. This indicated an awareness of the different perspectives and of the need to move forward more respectfully and with more alignment.

Phrases like 'from what I understand...', 'am I correct in thinking...' and 'is everyone in agreement about that?' characterised the sensitive nature of the senior leadership team interactions during this phase. Directors would be hesitant in giving an opinion, and then readily defer to the CEO or someone else if a differing perspective was detected, so there was still evidence of a lack of confidence in knowing how to progress.

The director team had just been through a series of 'team building' sessions before the COO arrived, clearly designed to assist with developing more open communication and transparency in the team following the difficult period of dissent. These sessions had provided them with the strategies to ensure communication remained constructive, and they were clearly using these tools to assist with navigating the fragile relationships.

Through the interviews, at this time the directors all indicated in different ways that they were hoping to see a more strategic and stable approach to growth and development.

An alternative approach to innovation is legitimised

During this research period, actions were also taken by the new COO to address the apparent challenges and try to rebalance. The most important of these actions included a targeted 'scenario planning' program, with a working group preparing for internal senior leadership team and board presentations, and budget planning sessions.

A 'technology roadmap' was also developed by the COO, with the introduction of new systems and structures to improve communication and consistency, such as new monthly staff development days and monthly day-long senior leadership team meetings. There was a shift to SharePoint and a Google Docs platform was introduced, along with the development of a new online learning platform that would help to save time and limit potential duplication of effort.

Initial evidence of a distinctive shift from the 'chaos' and 'siloed' positions became apparent as leaders started to identify and align with distinct emergent sensemaking orientations that came to be represented by the two most senior executive positions in the organisation: the CEO and COO. The two predominant sensemaking orientations that could be identified after the COO's arrival, and that persevered over the period of study, were identified as:

1 Contributing to the image of the organisation as a grassroots movement, with passion driving innovative, courageous, responsive, exploratory actions and decisions – as represented by the CEO
2 Contributing to the image of the organisation as a larger more structured organisation and/or social enterprise (more financially sustainable) and a professional service, with the need for stability, consistency and control – as represented by the COO

Analysis of the language used by and in relation to the CEO and COO and the relevant actions revealed the nature of the tensions between the two perspectives and demonstrated the potential impact on strategic positions. The language was then shared in the senior leadership team as different senior leadership team members picked up on the emergent contrasting perspectives and aligned themselves with one orientation or the other.

A number of the new senior leadership team members appointed after the crisis aligned directly with the founding CEO's position, having been promoted into the position due to their loyalty to the 'responsive, passionate, innovative' story or having been recruited in recognition of their commitment to the cause, and therefore they recognised the importance of the core established mission of the organisation. The establishment of the new complementary executive position, with the appointment of the COO, indicated there were already concerns about the need for an alternative polar position that could adequately address the need for 'control and efficiency'.

The COO was able to legitimise the polar position the role came to represent and establish an acceptable oppositional stance. Although the COO used language that characterised the elements of both perspectives, there was a demonstrated understanding of the need to take the oppositional polar position to the CEO to provide a counterbalance. As the COO explained 'I was brought in to be the ying to the CEO's yang', and the drawing of this was a striking representation of this principle.

The COO determined that deliberately taking this position would help to provide a solid platform for more sustainable innovation and growth. At this time, there was a clear shift in allegiance from a number of the senior leadership team away from the CEO and the 'responsive, passionate, innovative' sensemaking orientation to the desire for a more 'strategic' focus through a growing acceptance of the COO's 'efficiency, control, consolidation' orientation.

Leaders recognise and accept the innovation paradox

One director, who had been with the organisation for an extended period of time and had previously been fiercely loyal to the CEO and the CEO's vision, affirmed that the crisis 'really made me see how process is really important in making sure that we're being flexible, but, at the same time, making sure that with a little process it is really essential to making sure that we keep this organisation going'. This director reflected that at the time of the crisis, the organisation had been 'ripe for that kind of thing to happen, where people could question the organisation, when we don't have consistent procedures and processes'. Statements like these demonstrated a growing paradoxical awareness in the senior leadership team as they learnt to recognise the value and importance of both perspectives.

Once they appreciated that an alternative valid perspective had been established, senior leadership team members went through a period of testing and adjusting to find ways to keep the balance while shifting to embrace important aspects of the 'efficiency. control, consolidation' sensemaking orientation and hold the tensions between the two polar positions.

The general way allegiances and alliances started to shift over the research period is shown in the visual representation in Figure 4.4. This graphic shows the changes in the formal roles according to the organisation chart before the arrival of the COO (Figure 4.4A) and after the arrival of the COO (Figure 4.4B), illustrating the changing informal communication channels that became evident during this transition period.

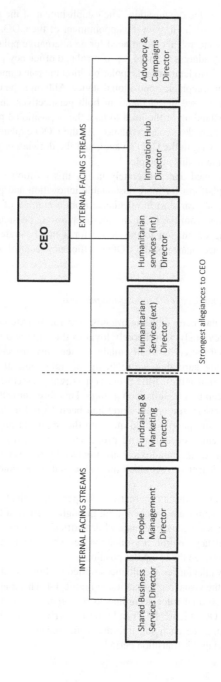

A. Formal organisaton chart before the COO started

Figure 4.4 Organisation chart showing formal roles and informal shifts in allegiances

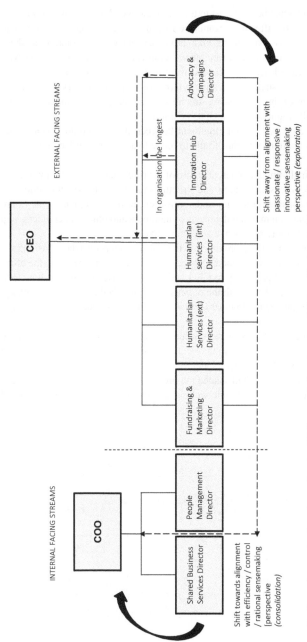

EXTERNAL FACING STREAMS

INTERNAL FACING STREAMS

CEO

COO

Advocacy & Campaigns Director

Innovation Hub Director

Humanitarian services (int) Director

Humanitarian Services (ext) Director

Fundraising & Marketing Director

People Management Director

Shared Business Services Director

In organisation the longest

Shift away from alignment with passionate / responsive / innovative sensemaking perspective *(exploration)*

Shift towards alignment with efficiency / control / rational sensemaking perspective [*consolidation*]

B. Formal organisation chart after the COO started also showing shifting allegiances (dotted lines)

Those who had been closest to the CEO and who had been with him since the start or soon after the organisation began tended to remain more loyal to the 'responsive, passionate, innovative' sensemaking orientation, as these people were also in external member facing roles and more in contact with members' critical needs. Staff who were newest to the organisation or who were the most distant (physically, in terms of location of work desk, and in role, in terms of 'internal' facing streams rather than 'external' facing streams) more readily aligned with the COO position.

Strategic consensus and alignment between the two predominant sensemaking orientations was thus found to relate to a few critical factors:

1 Role – including the inherent nature of the role, such as is it an 'inward facing' role (focus on systems and structures to support the organisation, so a need to consider efficiency and control) or an 'outward facing' role (more direct focus on meeting the needs of members and other stakeholders, so a need to be more responsive and innovative)
2 Proximity – including proximity to the SSO members on a daily basis, physical proximity to CEO and COO according to physical location in the office and emotional proximity to CEO and COO historically, such as how long that person has been with the organisation and whether they were with the organisation and the founder CEO in the early 'grassroots movement' days

Figure 4.5 reveals the positions of senior leadership team members in relation to the predominant sensemaking orientations and the relationship to the range of external contributing factors identified.

The founding CEO had shaped the predominant orientation in response to meeting the needs of the people seeking asylum in a rapidly changing political

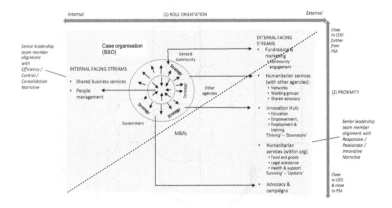

Figure 4.5 Range of factors related to senior leadership team alliances

context, yet the COO had managed to bring an alternative response and create a valid opposing position which was simultaneously both opposed to the original CEO position but also in alignment. This was represented by a shift to additional or alternative allegiance to an 'efficiency, control, consolidation' orientation, which provided a strong alternative yet equally important orientation, and which meant it had become valid to adopt both perspectives in pursuit of the organisation mission and purpose. The senior leadership team members had then aligned with the CEO's orientation and/or with the COO's alternative orientation, often according to their roles. Rather than operating at cross purposes, having a strong core purpose enabled them to hold the tension between the two opposing positions and to work in alignment through consensus.

Realignment around the innovation polar positions

After the validity of both polar positions was established by the executive leaders, the polar perspectives were then often adopted by different members of the senior leadership team. This meant that the team that eventually work as an organic whole in exhibiting the range of behaviours in this repertoire required for sustainable innovation and growth.

The data revealed that although there was constant movement in positions according to specific scenarios, different individual actors continued to gravitate towards one polar position on this continuum or the other according to roles and allegiances. Most could, however, eventually appreciate the value of both positions. All individuals in the senior leadership team had strong values and a clear commitment to the cause, but they came to recognise there could be differences in how this vision could be enacted and that they could embrace both perspectives. This growing awareness impacted their collective behaviours and strategic decisions.

An example of the way respect and trust for the polar orientations was developing could be seen in the way the fundraising role was managed. The CEO had taken over the role following the departure of the previous fundraising director during the crisis period. The CEO believed this was of critical importance for the future of the organisation, so had initially taken full responsibility for the position. Despite advertising a few times, no one suitable was found, so the CEO stretched to continue in the role. The COO stated at the time that the CEO may not have trusted anyone enough to take over this important position.

The first indication that there might be growing trust and acceptance of the need for a professional to take over this role from the CEO was when a new fundraising director was appointed who had been recommended by the COO. The fundraising director recognised the focus would be on ensuring financial stability for the organisation over the long term and, having come from a background in working with both corporates and not-for-profits, this director was passionate about the cause but also pragmatic about how to set and reach strategic fundraising goals.

The fundraising director was initially keen to introduce a more professional approach to fundraising, including conducting more stringent research-based market research and hiring professionals to call up donors to solicit donations. The CEO was open to the idea of a more professional approach through market research, but highly resistant to the idea of having professional fundraisers calling donors. The director and the rest of the team soon learned that this was a non-negotiable for the CEO and, although they did not all agree, they eventually all accepted these wishes because they recognised it was a critical strategic value that had been core to the organisation's purpose.

The team soon learned that they could take 'anti-parallel' positions in relation to other issues that were more negotiable for the CEO.

Developing an integrated innovation practice

Towards the end of the study, it was evident that a number of the team accepted the 'new normal' state, which clearly required some sort of dynamic balancing between the two polar positions of 'innovation at all costs' to reach the maximum number of clients and 'ensuring stability, efficiency and effectiveness' for long-term sustainability and survival.

The CEO summarised the general increasing awareness of the importance of finding a way of allowing both perspectives to coexist in harmony through the new strategic approach:

> *One of our challenges is that really complex dance between how do you make sure there's transparency, consistency and integrity in how you make decisions? But there's also innovation, and that's really hard... It's about how do you not become stifled and mediocre and safe, and how do you keep thriving and responding, and that's such an important thing that we do.*

The deepening commitment to the core principles of the organisation and practical strategic alignment around the new integrated story was demonstrated in the way mutual agreement was finally reached regarding the growth challenge. As the CEO continued to seek expansion in the mission to respond to client needs, there was a persistence in setting growth goals beyond the current model.

It had become clear to everyone in the senior leadership team that whereas the purpose (as exemplified by the passionate CEO in the early days) had at first provided a cohesive glue for the small start-up team, as the organisation grew there was less clarity around how the purpose could be strategically achieved. Most senior leadership team members could recognise that, as the scope of the organisation rapidly grew and the number of staff, volunteers and members increased, the limited awareness of how to achieve alignment around the purpose was not sufficient to keep everyone together.

There had been a conceptual reversal in the power generated by the drive to achieve the mission of the organisation, which had been propelling the organisation forward to this point. This had, however, become a destructive force as different interpretations of how to achieve this mission emerged.

Rallying around a shared integrated story

The strong core purpose had always been a critical factor driving the leadership team, but it was only once a more balanced approach to innovation was established the core purpose could help to hold the disparate threads together.

As the CEO identified:

> *We're trying to build a movement, that is, we're trying to rally around a shared sense of values and purpose... and represent a welcoming sanctuary and hope for people who seek our protection... Fifteen years later it never gets easy, and, as a leader, you always keep pushing for even greater excellence, you keep innovating.*

There had already been several phases of transition in the sizes and locations of the properties housing the organisation, including from a small shopfront property to a 3,000-square metre purpose-built warehouse-style property to an additional satellite office in another town in the same state. The next stage of the CEO's plan had been to set up representative offices in two more states across the country, and then to look into arranging for the organisation to take on a much broader regional role through establishing a regional office.

Recognising how all this was stretching the team, and with concerns for the capability of the current systems and structures to support such rapid and broad expansion, the COO and a number of directors sought 'growth through consolidation' as a strategic goal. A fascinating observation was that this was an inherently paradoxical approach – to be pursuing both growth and consolidation at the same time! The integrated story that emerged, which maintained a responsive passionate focus while simultaneously recognising the need to be selective about how this was done, was rapidly taken on board by the whole director team. This became apparent as they started using language that indicated alignment. For example, workshops focused on not only what teams should 'start' or 'continue' doing but also what they should 'stop' doing.

One of the major realisations during this period was that rather than trying to be everything to everyone, and rather than feeling the need to rapidly physically expand as a result, the organisation could start to have more of a resource coordination role through partnering with other organisations. This pivot demonstrated a significant win/win strategy, as it could extend the reach of the organisation without stretching people and resources beyond what was realistic and sensible. This strategy revealed a powerful alternative model for ensuring innovative yet sustainable organisation development.

The 'growth through consolidation' principle in practice

A simple example of how this integrated 'growth through consolidation' strategy became enacted in practice could be observed in a decision the Director of the Innovation Hub had made on the use of a customised 'driving instruction' car after consultation with the senior leadership team. This car had been donated to the Hub to provide vulnerable clients with driving lessons to increase their opportunities for social connections and teach them a skill that may help gain employment.

The car had already been specially adapted for this purpose at a cost, with dual operating features for driving instructors. Yet the team in the Hub had felt too stretched to cover this role properly, and the maintenance costs were adding up. Despite wanting to keep providing this service for their clients, a cost-benefit analysis revealed that the car could be sold and the money better put to use by providing members with driving lesson vouchers through established driving instruction companies, with an associated saving also in the team's time and energy.

Similarly, a 'food truck justice' project, which had been recognised as a highly innovative new project and had been the focus of a great deal of media attention for fundraising, was rationalised after it was assessed that it was not financially viable over the long term. This truck was designed to travel to areas where clients were located at a distance from the food supplies available at the SSO centre.

Although it was a popular project that donors liked to support, a critical assessment by the humanitarian services team revealed that the food truck project was not able to provide enough assistance to the communities it sought to help to justify continuing the service. The senior leadership team had been concerned about how they could notify the loyal donors who had contributed especially to this project, but once the decision was made that the best course of action was to close down the project they soon learnt that the donors were completely understanding and supportive of the decision.

Another even more significant opportunity to find synergy between the 'innovative, responsive, growth' and 'efficiency, control' sensemaking orientations through an integrated 'consolidation' story emerged when options for expanding the new satellite office were considered. A larger premise had already been selected for the move, and there had been plans to offer additional services with the space available. The senior leadership team was concerned with how they would cope with managing the larger premises and additional programs requiring more employees and volunteers. With a number of the directors now thinking in terms of consolidation in alignment with the COO's perspective, the 'anti-parallel' position to the 'growth at all costs' strategy was taken into account.

Rather than aiming to set up additional services and potentially duplicate the good work other not-for-profit organisations were doing in the same area, the idea was floated that this space could become an opportunity to set up a new 'integrated services' model. This idea was thoroughly researched and developed, and it was identified that in New Zealand a 'service innovation working group' had successfully established such an 'integrated services' model.

As information about this model reveals:

> Integrated services is about joining up... services around key events in people's lives [life events] to make it easier for citizens to access... [these] services. A key part of the integrated services design process is about exploring people's needs outside of the limitations of any single product, service, agency or sector.[2]

The senior leadership team realised that this model would be an opportune way to meet both the 'growth' and 'consolidation' needs simultaneously. The final solution involved asking for 'expressions of interest' from established organisations already offering professional standard services in the area who could complement the work SSO was doing and help to fill the gaps, and then planning to house these complementary services in the new building alongside the current SSO services.

One organisation for each complementary role was selected to take an office in the new space, and SSO's role was to run the reception area and greet clients as they arrived, to conduct a brief case consultation to identify the needs of the client and to coordinate visits to the other trusted providers in the centre and oversee database management. The new integrated system was designed to make the experience easier and less stressful for people in need and at the same time it made the staff's work easier.

Productive innovation alignment

The general outcome of finding ways to integrate both perspectives was much greater working alignment in the senior leadership team, despite the clear oppositional differences – or, more specifically, because of a clear understanding of how the differences could be used to an advantage through working together in synergy. As one director expressed:

> *I really feel like this team is quite aligned and connected, and I think we're all very committed to achieving the goals together. I really feel like we're all on the same page, and even though we disagree or have different perspectives or whatever, I do feel like every single person in this room has the core values of the (organisation) at heart, whether we agree, or we don't. We all had different perspectives (before), but I really feel like they all understand why we're here, and that's why I'm happy with robust discussion, because of that. I definitely don't think it's about ego or people trying to get ahead... I really do feel like it's all about the core values of the organisation and that's much nicer than we've experienced before.*

The practical consequences of the new integrated alignment was further highlighted in another director's comment at this time:

> *We're actually doing what we're meant to be doing, not trying to find the fly in the ointment, and then blame someone for that fly, and that's what my experience was with this particular group of people (during the crisis). It's very different. It's almost like chalk and cheese. So, I know we've still got a long way to go, but just the fact that people really care about their job, they care about the people that they work for, that we're all in it together, that we're trying really hard. We might disagree on points, but I think everyone really knows what the core intention is. It's our members that are the most important, it's the work, it's about making sure that we keep this organisation thriving, so that we can keep doing the work that we're doing, and I think that that is a massive change, you know? Whereas before it was just so toxic, really toxic.*

As the CEO summarised:

> *When your culture and your values and your trust and all those things are challenged, it's always about what have you learned from it and how do you come up stronger from it and how do you stay true to your mission and your purpose. I think the way in which we've been able to rebuild the team and trust and the way in which we've been able to thrive and succeed has been about going back to basics... In the last staff survey results my senior leadership team ranked in the top 3% for comparative organisations, and they were impressed to have 100% alignment. That's a lot of hard work, that was a year of hard work to get to that point... We've been putting a good 15 months of work, as a leadership team, to learn and to be strong.*

The insights into 'the way we've been able to thrive and succeed' in order to reach '100% alignment' provides valuable information on how to make sense of paradoxical tensions in innovation contexts. Indications that the senior leadership team found effective strategies to negotiate differences and achieve consensus through shared stories are that SSO appears to have emerged from the challenges of the crisis (or as one director described, rising 'from the ashes') and moved forward constructively, and the current senior leadership team formed a united and cohesive team as expressed by all team members.

The findings of the study demonstrate how the 'purpose-driven' mission of the organisation can inadvertently result in divisive and destructive outcomes for the senior leadership team or, conversely, enable deep integrated strategic results from competing demands – depending on how the organisation's vision, mission and values are interpreted, communicated and implemented.

REFLECTION AND ACTION QUESTIONS

Reflection

- Why were rapid-change and growth important elements to consider in this case study?
- How was the crisis situation resolved? What were the three phases the organisation went through once there was a recognition that the chaos and innovation disruption needed to be dealt with, and why was each phase significant?
- What was the role of collective paradoxical cognition in ensuring future sustainable innovation?
- How did a shared integrated narrative help to bring innovation alignment for the leadership team?

Action

- For the study or work scenario identified in the Reflection Questions from Chapter 2, consider:

  - What relevant background factors would need to be taken into account? Why?
  - Have you considered both internal and external factors?

- Look back at your sensemaking notes or drawings from the Chapter 3 Reflection Questions. Can you see a pattern in the actions and reactions that indicates phases of transition or development? Record any ideas that emerge from thinking this through.

Notes

1 Byrne and Ragin, 2009
2 DTA, 2019

References

Byrne, D., & Ragin, C. C. (2009). *The Sage handbook of case-based methods*. Thousand Oaks: Sage Publications.

Digital Transformation Agency (DTA). (2019). Australian government digital transformation agency. https://www.dta.gov.au/digital-transformation-strategy/three-strategic-priorities/government-thats-easy-deal/integrated-services-supporting-your-needs-and-life-events

5 New thinking in action

Practical purpose-driven innovation insights and applications

---

OVERVIEW

This chapter explores ***actionable insights and practical applications*** from the research.

Identifying the impact of tensions as an organisation deals with rapid change and/or scales-up is an important first step. Similarly, it is important to accept and address the particular challenges of small entrepreneurial start-ups that begin with a single founder/leader and rapidly transition to become larger more established organisations.

The role of the sensemaking process and how this can contribute to creating an organisation culture was found to be important in this research, as it was identified that introducing and modelling a new narrative based on a shared purpose through 'sensegiving' can be a critical strategy for success.

The practices that enable sustainable innovation growth have been identified as: (1) *channelling divergence* – or finding the diverse reasons for chaos and the source of innovation disruption; (2) *validation of*

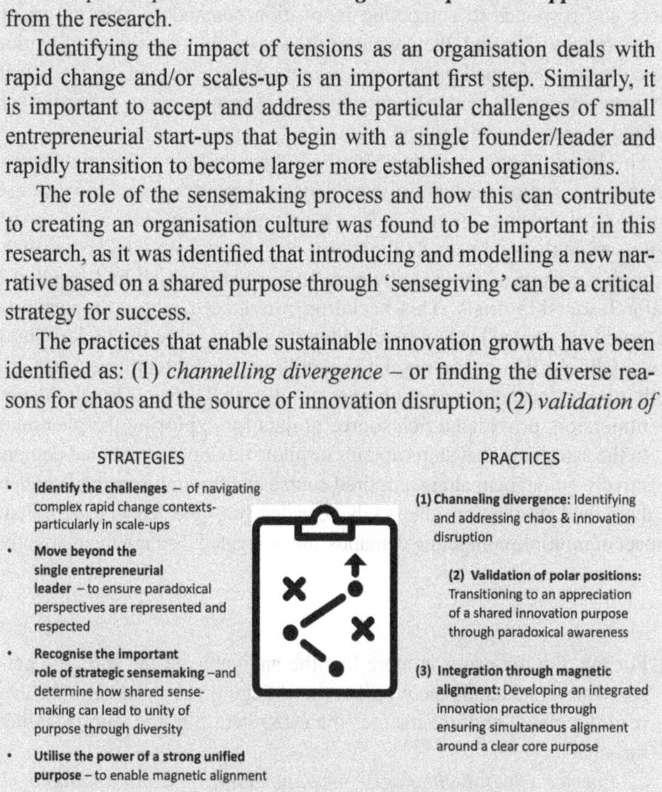

STRATEGIES	PRACTICES
• **Identify the challenges** – of navigating complex rapid change contexts- particularly in scale-ups	**(1) Channeling divergence:** Identifying and addressing chaos & innovation disruption
• **Move beyond the single entrepreneurial leader** – to ensure paradoxical perspectives are represented and respected	**(2) Validation of polar positions:** Transitioning to an appreciation of a shared innovation purpose through paradoxical awareness
• **Recognise the important role of strategic sensemaking** –and determine how shared sense-making can lead to unity of purpose through diversity	**(3) Integration through magnetic alignment:** Developing an integrated innovation practice through ensuring simultaneous alignment around a clear core purpose
• **Utilise the power of a strong unified purpose** – to enable magnetic alignment	

Figure 5.1 New insights and applications for purpose-driven innovation leadership

DOI: 10.4324/9781003426691-5

polar positions – or developing paradoxical cognition through revealing the power and process of incorporating apparently contradictory yet equally valid innovation perspectives of breakthrough innovation plus incremental innovation; and (3) *integration through magnetic alignment* – or ensuring a clear core purpose and mission that incorporates the paradoxical innovation positions (Figure 5.1).

Navigating the scaling-up process

Senior leaders play a significant role in determining and implementing an organisation's strategy. Understanding the way senior leadership teams deal with competing demands in the innovation context is therefore critical for understanding how to support effective innovation and growth.

This study focused on identifying how a senior leadership team experiences and responds to competing innovation demands within an organisation's strategy. Through the course of the study, the importance of exploring the collective sensemaking process in more detail emerged, so investigating the intricacies of the senior leadership team dynamics in the collective sensemaking process became a focal point.

The longitudinal case study methodology provided the opportunity to observe the senior leadership team sensemaking processes in response to paradoxical tensions in action. The case organisation was a not-for-profit organisation that had been deliberately selected because it had recently been through a period of rapid innovation and growth, which had resulted in a major leadership crisis. This backdrop provided a unique opportunity to observe how senior leaders would identify and manage the underlying tensions. Observation of the regular naturally occurring team meetings, along with other informal observation opportunities that arose through the period of immersion, provided a rich source of data for exploring the phenomena.

In the same way that ship captains or pilots rely on navigational equipment to actively guide them along a desired course and through potential challenges to their final destination, this study revealed how the leaders identified the impact of multiple competing demands and navigated through them effectively.

For me, the innovator is more like the navigator on the ship, the person who understands the weather, the changing environment, who can read the charts and understands the ecosystem that the ship is sailing through.

Former Chief Technologist for Innovation of a multinational IT company

The journey from start-up to scale-up is inevitably volatile, and few scale-up leaders survive this journey unscathed.[1] The rapid pace of growth and change means that 'there will always be a gap between the demands of the high-growth enterprise and the structures and systems that are in place to manage its activities'.[2] So identifying how to navigate the fragile balance between competing innovation demands is particularly essential for rapid-growth enterprises.

As the unique scale-up tensions can lead to significant challenges for enterprise leaders and their teams,[3] a key task for enterprise leaders will be how to manage these challenges[4] and deal with the related competing demands.[5] To give an example, when it comes to risk taking, there can be a tension related to the ambiguity behind the need to take risks to innovate and fulfil the enterprise purpose and the need to avoid risks or only take carefully calculated risks to ensure enterprise survival.

Enterprises that learn to self-organise have been found to be able to ensure they can remain innovative and flexible to respond to emerging needs as well as being able to ensure they can organise and construct enough order to ensure stability for dealing with day-to-day requirements.[6] Yet few enterprises self-organise effectively to manage the scale-up tensions effectively and survive the challenges.[7]

Additionally, due to the speed of growth and developing maturity, scale-ups are also more prone to change the environmental context they operate within through leadership changes,[8] which can be destabilising. There is therefore a need to better understand how leaders can better navigate the scale-up process to help prepare them better prepare them for it, and in this research I identified some practical strategies through consulting with the literature, leveraging the empirical data collected, building on theory, and determining business applications.

Unique leadership needs

As leadership requirements will be distinctive through each of the scale-up phases, enterprise leaders need to develop an awareness of how these requirements can change. But little is known about how leaders can meet changing needs through adapting their goals and behaviours appropriately.

There is known to be a shift from the need for an exploration focus to an exploitation focus as the enterprise goes through a growth phase[9]; for example, yet the way this tension may manifest more specifically in scale-up enterprises and how it can be managed in this context is not known as well. Leadership for 'exploration' is associated with a focus on decentralisation, loose cultures and less formalised processes that enable experimentation – while the need for 'exploitation' is associated with more control and formalisation through capturing refinement, ensuring efficiency and enabling incremental improvements that succeed by reducing variance and increasing sustainability.[10]

Leaders of scale-ups cannot exclusively focus on future innovation and growth at the expense of dealing with current challenges and demands.[11] Moreover, these leaders cannot simply address current needs, as they must simultaneously identify and respond to potential future needs to both remain competitive and ensure survival.[12] Scale-up leaders must instead ensure longevity by developing behavioural repertoires that foster 'consistency, stability and control' which support exploitative functions, at the same time as ensuring innovative approaches through demonstrating 'passion, risk taking and creativity', which support exploratory functions.[13]

It can be difficult for scale-ups to maintain the type of rapid growth required to create value,[14] and as enterprise survival depends on the effective management of this tension,[15] it is clear that more research is needed into how enterprise leaders can adapt to and navigate the challenges of pursuing growth opportunities while building and maintaining stable structures to support the growth.[16]

Getting beyond the single entrepreneurial founder

Scale-ups are likely to experience a 'crisis of leadership' from the tensions of dealing with competing demands.[17] Organisation design, team composition and enterprise culture have all been found to be impacted by the contradictory yet complementary narratives related to the competing demands of 'endurance' and 'change'.[18] Yet although most scale-ups operate with a single chief executive officer (CEO) founder at the helm, few individual entrepreneurial leaders are ready or equipped for dealing with these scale-up challenges.[19]

Young organisations with a focus on growth through innovative strategies and actions, known as 'entrepreneurial enterprises', are often started and led by single entrepreneurial founders,[20] so understanding how these entrepreneurial leaders might address the scale-up tensions is critical. The entrepreneurial leaders who may be well suited to starting a new enterprise are typically action-oriented risk-takers[21] with a strong growth orientation, ambition and an independent drive.[22] They aspire for growth through innovation[23] and have a 'preference for creating activity'.[24] It might therefore be expected to follow that entrepreneurs would be well positioned to drive the innovation required for an enterprise scale-up, and indeed many entrepreneurs thrive and succeed significantly in the start-up phase or when a new phase of scale-up begins. But the 'internal locus of control, need for independence, need for responsibility, and need for power' associated with entrepreneurs can provide an additional challenge for scaling up successfully.[25]

The reality is that entrepreneurs are often 'visionary and innovation-oriented, with a clear focus on creating new opportunities... tolerat(ing) chaos and a lack of structure'.[26] They tend to operate at a faster pace in a non-consistent way on non-routine activities,[27] which can hinder a strategic and sustainable approach to growth. Additionally, the required entrepreneurial behaviours will change as the organisation grows from launching the new enterprise based on an innovative new idea through to operationally managing the emerging enterprise according to required performance outcomes,[28] and entrepreneurs are not always equipped for this.

Entrepreneurs are often required to take on multiple roles as 'marketer, a sales representative, a public relations officer, a financial controller and so on, wearing many different hats simultaneously'.[29] Entrepreneurial enterprises are especially prone to this given the lack of resources, along with the founder/entrepreneur potentially finding it difficult to relinquish power and control. They will typically need to adapt their leadership style from individually growing and 'protecting' their enterprise to 'letting go' as the size of the organisation rapidly increases.[30]

Either these leaders lead through the growing pains when their skillsets and leadership styles are no longer the most appropriate, or they are replaced with leaders who may be able to manage the establishment phase better but lack the entrepreneurial vision or passion that likely made the organisation unique.[31]

When two or more heads are better than one

It is apparent that new leadership models are needed to assist with the transformation in enterprise and management practices during periods of rapid growth.[32] Emerging literature is therefore shifting from more static analyses to identifying the dynamic processes at play as an organisation scales up,[33] most notably through strategic entrepreneurship.[34]

It is now widely recognised that although unitary executive leadership may best enable the coordination of a single vision,[35] individual entrepreneurial enterprise leaders are not necessarily equipped to deal with complex rapid-change growth contexts.[36] In particular, it is not possible to match the complexity and pace of innovation and change through a single leadership approach,[37] and a single leadership style is not sufficient for promoting innovation[38] – as simple linear relationships between leadership and innovation do not exist.[39] It is not feasible for a single individual to manage the competing demands of innovation and management specifically associated with entrepreneurial enterprise growth,[40] and dealing with the multiple unique challenges of resource scarcity, higher risk levels and ambiguity embedded in a new enterprise[41] presents unique challenges for the single leader.

Alternatives to the single leader models often acknowledge the need to deal with the competing demands arising from addressing multiple complexities simultaneously,[42] and there is growing evidence that enterprises led by entrepreneurial teams rather than individual entrepreneurs experience more sustainable growth.[43] There has subsequently been a shift to examining alternative leadership models that might enable the simultaneous management of the competing demands inherent in the scale-up tensions, particularly distributed leadership models.[44]

A model for distributed leadership

Distributed leadership models have variously been referred to as 'shared leadership',[45] 'collective leadership',[46] 'collaborative leadership',[47] 'co-leadership'[48] and 'emergent leadership'[49] – and more specifically 'dispersed leadership'[50] and 'dual executive leadership'.[51] These models can be distinguished by a focus on leadership as a collective social process rather than being the responsibility of just one person.[52]

Though research on distributed leadership and senior leadership teams is prolific, the complexity of senior leadership team dynamics may make it difficult to interpret how competing demands are navigated. The challenges of diverse perspectives in senior leadership teams have been acknowledged in the literature,[53] and it has been found that diverse perspectives can arise from social categorisation,[54] communication issues[55] and interpersonal conflict.[56]

Additionally, where there is diversity, a similarity-distinctiveness identity tension often needs to be negotiated, particularly by senior leaders.[57] Focusing on the two most senior leaders who have the most power can help to narrow the focus and enable a clearer interpretation of dynamics.[58] Dual executive leadership models are now therefore being identified as useful models for understanding how senior leaders can navigate complex contexts.[59] These models have been used in a range of organisations, and it has been proposed that this shared leadership model may alleviate the challenges of resource depletion for individual leaders who focus on innovation and may reduce the role conflict associated with the competing demands of the different processes of idea generation and implementation.[60]

I anticipated that this model might provide a useful framework for leaders dealing with competing demands such as those present in the scale-up context. Despite a general interest in these models, and although the need has been identified for alternative leadership models to both the single CEO approach[61] and the general senior leadership team approach,[62] I identified that the dual executive leadership model still needs to be more extensively studied in contexts such as this.[63]

The important role of strategic sensemaking

This study found that the senior leadership team in this context was vulnerable to paradoxical tensions related to rapid change, resource limitations and plurality, and that the team was only eventually able to transcend these challenges through the development of a shared integrated story based on a core purpose deriving from clear core values.

I identified that there can be a shift from the sensemaking practice of *divergence* (where individual polar positions cause tension and are experienced as chaos and silos) to *validation* (where paradoxical polar positions are identified, respected and embraced) when a senior leadership team *makes sense of competing demands collectively and inclusively.*

Table 5.1 Principles identified for senior leadership team transition from surviving to thriving

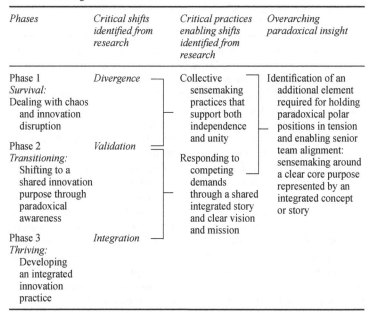

Phases	Critical shifts identified from research	Critical practices enabling shifts identified from research	Overarching paradoxical insight
Phase 1 *Survival:* Dealing with chaos and innovation disruption	Divergence	Collective sensemaking practices that support both independence and unity	Identification of an additional element required for holding paradoxical polar positions in tension and enabling senior team alignment: sensemaking around a clear core purpose represented by an integrated concept or story
Phase 2 *Transitioning:* Shifting to a shared innovation purpose through paradoxical awareness	Validation	Responding to competing demands through a shared integrated story and clear vision and mission	
Phase 3 *Thriving:* Developing an integrated innovation practice	Integration		

Further, there can be a shift from *validation* to *integration* (where paradoxical positions are embodied and pursued) when a senior leadership team *responds to the competing demands through a shared integrated story based on a strong purpose and clear vision and mission.*

The observed principles that enable the transition from chaos to alignment for a senior leadership team managing innovation and growth are outlined in Table 5.1. The pattern observed can be related to the need for resolution of a 'pragmatic paradox' or 'double bind'.[64] In this case, the leaders are expected to find new, effective solutions to support the SSO purpose (helping vulnerable clients), but they cannot do anything that challenges the role of the founder, who is inadvertently hindering the necessary adoption of innovation – as opposing the CEO (who represents SSO) would be seen as a betrayal of the organisation's purpose.

The leaders move from practices of formalism, isolation and withdrawal from engagement (in the *survival* phase) towards coping mechanisms that circumvent the previous paradox by creating 'autonomous mini-organizations' (in the *transition* phase), and finally overcoming the double bind and replacing it with manageable organising paradoxes than can then effectively be navigated (in the *thriving* phase).

The power of purpose for magnetic alignment

A unique overarching contribution of the research to paradox theory is the identification of *the role organisation attributes such as a strong core vision or purpose can play in bringing polar elements to the senior leader's attention*.

This finding builds on similar findings that emphasise the importance of a shared narrative,[65] but it was found in the current study that where purpose is framed as an *integrated* concept or story incorporating paradoxical polar positions simultaneously, as was evident in this study, the senior leader's attention can be drawn to the integrative aspects of the competing demands and the relatedness of polar elements can become salient.

For the integrated core vision to be an effective cohesive force, the inherent power dynamics at play (as represented by the differing alliances) and their potential to destabilise collective coherence must also be taken into account. Just as 'harmony' implies also dissonance, and a 'complex dance' consists of both resistance and compliance, this remains a messy process that must continue to be held in tension as it can never provide the opportunity for neat resolution. It is therefore important to create structural conditions for enabling a productive level of 'coopetition' (cooperation/competition) and overcoming the hegemonic conditions of the 'chaos' phase. Although discomfort with contradictory aspects of a vision or mission can split a senior leadership team, where certain elements exist at both the individual and organisational levels, it can be possible for more holistic approaches to emerge.[66] This research provided the opportunity to explore such elements further.

Additionally, while the interrelatedness of paradoxical tensions has been recognised in the literature,[67] there has been a further opportunity to build on prior findings to identify in more detail how elements identified may foster holistic responses. While there has often been a focus in paradox theory on outlining the nature of individual paradox pairs, this study helps to extend paradox theory by furthering our understanding of how the relational aspects of paradox pairs are enacted and enabled by senior leaders.

The study also demonstrates the importance of the leadership team being able to frame and communicate the purpose. Embodying paradoxical polar positions through a shared integrated story can provide a strong 'magnetic field' or compelling force to pull divergent elements into a dynamic *magnetic alignment*. This involves the acceptance of antithetical positions that appear to work in contrast to the magnetic core purpose, which helps to explain how paradoxes can be enacted in practice as both 'independent and interdependent'.[68]

Shared sensemaking for unity of purpose through diversity

An initial significant finding of the research was that *shared collective sensemaking practices that support innovation leadership involve shifts from divergence to validation and from validation to integration*, ultimately supporting collective senior team capabilities as a diverse yet cohesive team.

The results of this study show how tensions can emerge between sub-groups with divergent values[69] and conflict can erupt, particularly in complex transitioning organisations – even where there is apparently a common purpose and mission. This can be particularly evident at the leadership level, as the leaders' roles as both sensemakers and sensegivers in relation to followers need to be considered.[70]

Senior teams need to allow for variety yet facilitate collective action and strategic coherence.[71] Although it has been assumed in the past that unity can be established from sharing a common values and vision, which in turn can enable ambidexterity,[72] distinctiveness within the senior leadership team can 'shape how divergent views get expressed, interpreted, and worked through'.[73] Finding a balance between a sense of distinctiveness as individuals, on the one hand, and similarity as a senior leadership team, on the other, has therefore been found to be important in negotiating tensions over time.[74]

When a shared vision is acknowledged and accepted by a senior leadership team, it can help incorporate opposing views about tactical issues,[75] and specifically in relation to innovation,[76] but how this works in practice and how it can assist team alignment and coordinated team action has yet to be ascertained. Developing a strong shared integrated sensemaking concept or story can be a critical catalyst for surviving transition,[77] as identification with a social narrative can help to address the need people have for order and structure,[78] and to facilitate adaptation to change and commitment.[79]

For the case organisation, there was no immediate aligned configuration, but rather alignment could only be achieved through adoption of a series of practices. It was through collective sensemaking triggered by a significant crisis that it was possible for the senior leadership team members to identify the challenges and move through the exploratory development phases to achieve some sort of 'workable certainty'.[80]

While there has been an assumed focus in the literature in the past on how tensions from competing demands can be *resolved* in leadership teams,[81] the focus is now more on understanding how these tensions can be accepted and *valued*.[82] Valuation has been found to be a process of shaping and reshaping contexts[83] through emergent relational practices[84] that impact orientations and behaviours. Extending recent work in this area,[85] this research therefore further explored *how* senior leaders *work together collectively* to realise synergistic outcomes through subtle yet clear sensemaking shifts. The core practices observed and emergent principles identified in the research that enabled the strategic transition are outlined in Table 5.2.

Table 5.2 Sensemaking practices for transitioning from surviving to thriving

Temporal development	Characteristics of each phase	Core emergent sensemaking practices enabling transcendence of paradoxical competing demands
Background experience	• Crisis • Antagonistic relationships • Chaos	Divergence: *Characterised by unidentified polar positions, individual sensemaking & combative relationships*
Surviving Dealing with chaos and innovation disruption	• Divergent strategic perspectives • Multiple competing objectives • 'Artificial harmony' • Fragile relationships	
Transition Shifting to a shared innovation purpose through paradoxical awareness	• Validating alternative polar position established • Developing respect and trust • Shifting allegiances to alternative orientation (e.g. due to: • Role • Proximity to dominant voices (physical and emotional))	Validation: *Identifying, respecting and embracing paradoxical polar positions through developing collective sensemaking*
Moving towards thriving Developing an integrated innovation practice	• Desire for and introduction of more strategic development for both improved: • Roles and relationships • Systems and structures	Integration: *Embodying and pursuing paradoxical polar positions through a shared integrated story based on a strong purpose and clear vision and mission*

Although links to prior literature can be identified for each of these sense-making practices, the specific framing, processual pattern and outcomes were found to be unique through this research as follows.

Channeling divergence: dealing with chaos and innovation disruption

Where there is no paradoxical awareness, and where there is no acknowledge-ment or acceptance of the value of competing demands, individuals and teams tend to operate in silos. This research identified that this becomes a practice of 'divergence', as any sensemaking in this context is essentially independent and unrelated. If unchecked, this practice can lead to disconnection and dis-sent in a basic 'survival' mode.

Further challenges can become resentment and misalignment, ultimately resulting in destructive chaos. In this context, different polar orientations are likely to be experienced as irreconcilable tensions and grow into major sources of conflict, and the climate can easily become toxic and combative. The likely outcome with no intervention is a vicious cycle that is difficult to prevent.[86]

How to Deal with Innovation Divergence and Disruption

- Identify different individual reactions to change – who is more likely to embrace innovation and change, and who is more likely to feel threatened by it or be cautious about it? How can these differ-ences be acknowledged and addressed?
- Discuss the specific challenges that might be leading to tensions.
- Map team positions in response to new innovations.

Validation of polar position: transitioning to a shared innovation purpose through paradoxical awareness

The sensemaking practice that can break this negative cycle was identified in this research as 'validation'. Once oppositional polar positions are acknowl-edged and accepted through paradoxical cognition, there is the opportunity to find points of connection between different positions.

It is known that paradoxical cognition, or using frames and references that recognise and embrace contradiction, is critical for the strategic management of competing innovation demands.[87] In this research, it was identified that where at least one person in a leadership team demonstrates paradoxical cognition and is open to accepting points of connection between oppositional polar positions, this can become a foundation for building trust and respect – including encouraging more transparency and allowing for more alignment – even where there may be limited paradoxical cognition in the team as a whole.

This 'transition' mode involves a new emphasis on a relational approach, which supports the final shift to integration. Integration of two opposing positions simultaneously can then activate a form of collective 'transcendence'. While previous research has emphasised the importance of transcendence in managing paradoxical tensions[88] along with the role of collective sensemaking to enable individuals to move beyond a commitment to a particular frame,[89] this study contributes a collective relational sensemaking model that sheds light on how this can happen in practice.

This 'adaptive sensemaking' practice was found to be a responsive dynamic action which activates collective sensemaking and allows individuals to embrace the oppositional polar positions simultaneously. The research suggests that the establishment of two accepted polar positions which both fulfil the organisation purpose when addressed in tandem provides the opportunity for the differing orientations to align around that purpose.[90] The significant factor in this research was that, as well as having the same orientation as a dominant executive leader position (e.g. the position of the CEO), it can be valid to hold an oppositional position – as long as this position is also understood as being in alignment with the core purpose of the organisation. It can become accepted as valid, and in fact recognised as necessary, to adopt both polar perspectives in pursuit of the organisation mission and purpose.

The study found that a senior leadership team can thrive when their attention is drawn to the relational aspects of apparently contradictory competing demands in the organisation mission so that the organisation purpose can become an effective cohesive force. For the organisation, although a lack of clarity about how the organisation mission can best be fulfilled initially led to silos, disengagement and general disarray, where there is a magnetic field or clear core integrating purpose individuals can align around that field.

How to Enable Validation of a Shared Innovation Purpose

- Go back to the organisation vision, mission and values (VMV) – or put some work into further developing these to ensure they support the innovation paradoxes.
- Outline roles and responsibilities different individuals can take to support the polar innovation positions and in line with the VMV.
- Seek opportunities to initiate the development of trust and respect for different roles and responsibilities.

Integration through magnetic alignment: developing an integrated innovation practice

The practice of 'integration' was identified in this research as a means of combating innovation inertia.[91] This practice was found to involve the recognition of the need to strategically develop oppositional polar positions beyond the point of simple recognition of differences and the acceptance of them through synthesis.[92] The practice involves planning for the strategic development of both senior leadership team roles and relationships that enable ongoing collective sensemaking through the exploration processes, along with supporting systems and structures that enable exploitative and maintenance functions.

A senior leadership team can effect the principle of 'dynamic equilibrium' between two paradoxical polar positions[93] through using an integrated story as a shared sensemaking mechanism, which can enable synthesis between the paradoxical positions. In the case organisation, the practice involved the adoption of an integrated 'growth through consolidation' story that incorporated both perspectives. The ability of the senior leadership team to develop a shared story and negotiate these challenges is contingent on having opportunities to identify the underlying tensions, address the related issues and realign and retarget actions based on a return to the original vision – or, as in the case organisation, 'rally around a shared sense of values and purpose'.

Once there is integration, pursuing both simultaneously can sustain innovation and growth over the long term. An important finding of the research was that *the senior leadership team as a whole can embody and embrace these sensemaking practices through 'magnetic alignment' around an integrated core purpose.* In the same way that individual senior managers can achieve sustainable innovation by fostering both 'passion, risk taking and creativity', which support exploratory functions, and 'consistency, stability and control', which support exploitative functions,[94] a senior leadership team that includes individuals with these different orientations can also reach synergistic outcomes collectively.

Existing literature has focused on how individuals make sense of paradoxical tensions in a wide range of contexts, including in organisations where multiple logics exist, such as hybrid and transitioning organisations, but few studies have explored how behaviours and cognitive frames come together for senior leadership teams to reach shared consensus as a team in a growing organisation with competing demands.[95] As an example, a case study of a hybrid organisation identified that people in these organisations, in particular, can start to show a 'collective form of behavioural complexity through... more creative and dynamic synthesis across (different) logics'.[96] This study found that the people in the case organisation 'directly confronted and accepted the ambiguities involved in paradoxical outcomes, and they explicitly articulated a more complex framing of the (organisation's) identity as a catalyst', which is consistent with the findings from this study.

This study has, however, also included a more intensive exploration of these dynamics by focusing on the specific elements of individual and team experience that can arise in these contexts, and through identifying how this can impact team strategy. The research revealed that where awareness, respect and trust were simultaneously evident, alignment by the members of the senior leadership team with opposing polar sensemaking orientations was not a barrier to synergistic development. This practice involved confronting and accepting the ambiguities of opposing sensemaking orientations in the introduction of a validated counterbalance position, along with an increasing recognition that polar positions could simultaneously be pursued and held in tension.

Just as a strong magnetic field can provide a unifying force to bring divergent particles into alignment, members of senior leadership teams with opposing orientations can also find alignment and reach consensus where there is some awareness of the paradoxical nature of the organisation purpose and its relational role in holding everything together. This is most likely to happen where there is an appreciation of how opposing orientations can be brought together through an integrated shared concept or story to 'rally around'. The key principles identified for achieving aligned strategic objectives in the senior leadership team can be illustrated by referring to the integrative physics principle of 'magnetic dipoles', as shown in Figure 5.2.

An important implication is that it can be difficult to align individual efforts in a senior leadership team where individuals are operating independently. Where there is a recognition of a strong purpose that functions as the 'large external magnetic field', however, opposing paradoxical orientations arising from competing demands can be held in tension and can equally contribute to the greater purpose. Though a number of theorists have argued that in work situations 'what is shared between people are actions, activities, moments of conversation and joint tasks, not "meaning"',[97] this research identified that meaning and 'a shared sense of purpose' may be constructed and shared where purpose is central to the most senior leader's or organisation's identity. When the inevitable tensions between opposing orientations are confronted and the importance of strategic alignment is recognised, and when there is respect for the value of each position and the contribution to the greater good, it can be possible to find strategic alignment.

Although a strong core purpose can at first provide a cohesive glue for a small start-up team, as an organisation grows there needs to be clarity around how the purpose can be strategically achieved. In order to best manage the 'complex dance' between polar perspectives, a deep understanding of how the values and purpose could be interpreted and enacted in practice in a diverse team was required. As the competing demands multiply the tensions may be experienced as being pulled in a range of different directions and may lead to different outcomes.

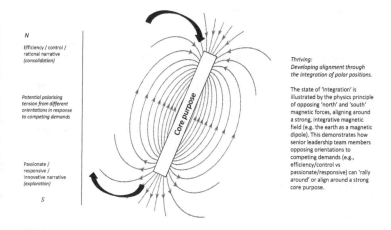

N

Efficiency / control /
rational narrative
(consolidation)

Potential polarising
tension from different
orientations in response
to competing demands

Passionate /
responsive /
innovative narrative
(exploration)

S

Thriving:
*Developing alignment through
the integration of polar positions.*

The state of 'integration' is
illustrated by the physics principle
of opposing 'north' and 'south'
magnetic forces, aligning around
a strong, integrative magnetic
field (e.g. the earth as a magnetic
dipole). This demonstrates how
senior leadership team members
opposing orientations to
competing demands (e.g.,
efficiency/control vs
passionate/responsive) can 'rally
around' or align around a strong
core purpose.

Figure 5.2 Magnetic alignment principles

Consider how there could be both a tension between the need to 'explore' and the need to 'preserve' when innovating and a tension between the need to ensure a focus on 'purpose' and financial sustainability or 'profit'. This can lead to a potentially interactive effect as represented in the matrix (Table 5.3).

Table 5.3 Identifying outcomes from multiple competing purpose-driven innovation demands

	Profit	Purpose
Exploration	Opportunistic, entrepreneurial	Optimistic, idealistic
Preservation	Financially conservative, utilitarian	Purpose-driven pragmatic

The more tensions you can untangle from the knotted complexity of real-life scenarios,[97] the less clear and less predictable the outcomes will be. This research identified that dynamic equilibrium[98] can be reached only where there are practices in place for identifying tensions, confronting the issues and seeking alignment through embracing paradoxical perspectives. The metaphor of 'navigating' has been introduced in this context to illustrate how cognisant awareness of paradoxical tensions can assist with making sense of those tensions in this context.[99] This research further demonstrates how a shared integrated organisation story that has been effectively incorporated into organisation principles and practices can provide a guiding compass for alignment and cohesive strategic action.

How to Support Integrated Innovation Practice through 'Magnetic Alignment'

- Design plans for the strategic development of leadership team roles and relationships that enables ongoing collective sensemaking and exploration.
- Identify or design an integrated empowering central story based on a strong core purpose that incorporates both 'passion, risk taking and creativity' and 'consistency, stability and control'.
- Focus on establishing systems to support the ongoing development of awareness, respect and trust to help ensure clear alignment.

The study therefore provides a better understanding of how senior leadership teams achieve strategic alignment around core values and purpose even from divergent paradoxical positions, which can enable a shift from surviving to transitioning and thriving through more strategic alignment. Understanding the process of how the team has reached collaborative alignment after a difficult period of transition contributes to our knowledge of how intentional change management strategies can be employed to help successfully navigate paradoxical tensions related to organisation transition at the senior leadership team level.

The research has revealed how it is possible to bring individuals with diverse backgrounds and experiences together (and therefore diverse perspectives, emotions and cognitive frames) to reach shared consensus in the context of organisations with divergent strategic objectives and multiple logics.

REFLECTION AND ACTION QUESTIONS

Reflection

- How important do you think leadership dynamics are for organisations wishing to innovate for purpose? Why?
- If you were a consultant for a for-purpose organisation with an entrepreneurial founder leader and a desire to expand, what would you recommend based on the insights revealed in this chapter? What would you recommend specifically to:

  - The entrepreneurial leader
  - The board
  - The leadership team

- How could you ensure a proactive rather than reactive approach is taken?

Action

- For the study or work scenario you identified in the Reflection Questions from Chapter 2, consider:

  - Can you identify any period of chaos and/or innovation disruption? If so, how did it manifest and what was the impact for all stakeholders involved?
  - What was the turning point – how and why did things change? Did they change for the better or for worse? Why?
  - Was there any fallout apparent from a period of rapid change or growth?

- What are the two polar positions that need to be addressed to navigate the challenge successfully?
- What new conceptual illustration and/or and narrative could integrate these polar positions effectively and help to provide a shared core purpose and a framework for mutual understanding?
- If you were a consultant for the case you have been asked to explore, how would you recommend the key stakeholders enact the following principles:

  - Channel divergence
  - Validate the polar positions
  - Integrate these polar positions through magnetic alignment

Notes

1 Antonakis and Autio, 2014, Ensley et al., 2006, Mueller et al. 2013
2 Nicholls-Nixon, 2005, p. 85
3 Ashforth and Reingen, 2014, Battilana and Dorado, 2010, Besharov, 2014, Jay, 2013, Tracey et al., 2011
4 Morris, Zahra, and Schindehutte 2000
5 Simsek et al., 2015, Poole and Van de Ven, 2004
6 Drazin and Sandelands, 1992, Stacey, 1995
7 Stanford, 2007
8 Ensley et al., 2006
9 Mueller et al., 2013
10 Benner and Tushman, 2003, Jansen et al., 2008, Knight and Harvey, 2015, March, 1991; Papachroni et al., 2016, Smith and Tushman, 2005, Tushman and O'Reilly, 1996
11 Bansal, 2002
12 Hahn et al., 2014, Mom et al., 2007
13 Jansen et al., 2009, p. 7
14 Jansen and Roelofsen, 2018, Josefy et al., 2015
15 Adler and Obstfeld, 2007
16 Simsek et al., 2015
17 Greiner, 1989, Cope et al., 2011

18 DeSantola and Gulati, 2017
19 Mueller et al., 2013
20 Carland et al., 1984, Schumpeter, 1934
21 d'Amboise and Muldowney, 1988
22 Wasserman, 2003
23 Simsek et al., 2018
24 Carland et al., 1984, p. 357
25 Carland et al., 1984, p. 357
26 Probst et al., 2011, p. 331
27 Casson, 2000
28 Naffziger et al., 1994
29 Cope et al., 2011, p. 270
30 Cope et al., 2011
31 Wasserman, 2003
32 Zahra et al., 2006
33 Coad et al., 2017
34 Hitt et al., 2011
35 Alvarez and Svejenova, 2005, Fayol, 1949, Mintzberg, 1979
36 Heenan and Bennis, 1999
37 Ancona et al., 2001
38 Rosing et al., 2011
39 Mitchell and James, 2001
40 Alvarez et al., 2007, Mumford and Hunter, 2005
41 Ensley et al., 2003, Morris and Zahra, 2000
42 Reid and Karambaya, 2009
43 Gimmon, 2008, Harper, 2008, Lechler, 2001, Vyakarnam and Handelberg, 2005
44 Bolden, 2011
45 Pearce and Conger, 2003
46 e.g. Denis et al., 2001
47 e.g. Rosenthal, 1998
48 e.g. Heenan and Bennis, 1999
49 e.g. Beck, 1981
50 Ray et al., 2004
51 Reid and Karambayya, 2009
52 Barker, 2001, Hosking, 1988
53 Alvarez and Svejenova, 2005, Locke, 2003, Pearce et al., 2007
54 Tajfel, 1982
55 Auh and Menguc, 2005
56 Amason, 1996, Knight et al., 1999
57 Cuganesan, 2017
58 Hunter et al., 2017
59 Lukoschek et al., 2018
60 Hunter et al., 2017
61 Alvarez et al., 2007, Mumford and Hunter, 2005
62 Ping et al., 2016
63 Huq et al., 2017
64 Tracy, 2004, Watzlawick, Beavin and Jackson, 1967
65 eg Abdallah, Denis and Langley, 2011, Bednarek, Paroutis and Sillince, 2017
66 Ashforth and Reingen, 2014
67 Cuganesan, 2017, Jarzabkowski, Lê and Van de Ven, 2013, Lüscher and Lewis, 2008
68 Smith and Lewis, 2011
69 Pratt and Rafaeli, 1997

70 Sparr, 2018
71 O'Reilly and Tushman, 2004
72 Heavey and Simsek, 2017, Raisch and Birkinshaw, 2008
73 Knight and Cuganesan, 2019, p. 23
74 Cuganesan, 2017
75 Simons, Pelled and Smith, 1999
76 Jansen et al., 2008, Orton and Weick, 1990
77 Albert, Ashforth and Dutton, 2000
78 Hogg and Terry, 2000
79 Pfeffer, 1994
80 Lüscher and Lewis, 2008
81 O'Reilly and Tushman, 2013
82 as introduced by Andriopoulos and Lewis, 2009
83 Zimmermann, Raisch and Cardinal, 2018
84 Gehman, Treviño and Garud, 2013, Kornberger, 2017
85 Knight and Cuganesan, 2019, Knight and Paroutis, 2017, Papachroni, Heracleous and Paroutis, 2016
86 Andriopoulos and Lewis, 2009, Lewis, 2000, 2010, Smith and Lewis, 2011, Smith et al., 2017
87 Smith and Tushman, 2005
88 Abdallah, Denis and Langley, 2011, Lüscher and Lewis, 2008
89 Cornelissen, Mantere and Vaara, 2014
90 Jansen et al., 2008
91 Smith and Tushman, 2005
92 Poole and Van de Ven, 1989
93 Smith and Lewis, 2011
94 Jansen, Vera and Crossan, 2009
95 Hargrave and Van De Ven, 2017
96 Jay, 2013, p. 154
97 Sheep, Fairhurst and Khazanchi, 2017
98 Smith and Lewis, 2011
99 Jay, 2013, p. 147

References

Abdallah, C., Denis, J. L., & Langley, A. (2011). Having your cake and eating it too: Discourses of transcendence and their role in organizational change dynamics. *Journal of Organizational Change Management*, *24*(3), 333–348.

Adler, P. S., & Obstfeld, D. (2007). The role of affect in creative projects and exploratory search. *Industrial and Corporate Change*, *16*(1), 19–50.

Albert, S., Ashforth, B. E., & Dutton, J. E. (2000). Organizational identity and identification: Charting new waters and building new bridges., *Academy of Management Review*, *25*(1), 13–17.

Alvarez, S. A., & Barney, J. B. (2007). Discovery and creation: Alternative theories of entrepreneurial action. *Strategic entrepreneurship journal*, 1(1-2), 11–26.

Alvarez, J. L., & Svejenova, S. (2005). *Sharing executive power: Roles and relationships at the top.* Cambridge University Press.

Amason, A. C. (1996). Distinguishing the effects of functional and dysfunctional conflict on strategic decision making: Resolving a paradox for top management teams. *Academy of Management Journal*, *39*(1), 123–148.

112 *New thinking in action*

Ancona, D. G., Goodman, P. S., Lawrence, B. S., & Tushman, M. L. (2001). Time: A new research lens. *Academy of Management Review, 26*(4), 645–663.

Andriopoulos, C., & Lewis, M. W. (2009). Exploitation-exploration tensions and organizational ambidexterity: Managing paradoxes of innovation. *Organization Science, 20*(4), 696–717.

Antonakis, J., & Autio, E. (2014). Entrepreneurship and leadership. In J. R. Baum, R. A. Baron, R. J. Baum, and M. Frese, *The psychology of entrepreneurship* (pp. 221–240). United Kingdom: Psychology Press.

Ashforth, B. E., & Reingen, P. H. (2014). Functions of dysfunction: Managing the dynamics of an organizational duality in a natural food cooperative. *Administrative Science Quarterly, 53*(3), 474–516.

Auh, S., & Menguc, B. (2005). Balancing exploration and exploitation: The moderating role of competitive intensity. *Journal of Business Research, 58*(12), 1652–1661.

Bansal, P. (2002). The corporate challenges of sustainable development. *Academy of Management Perspectives, 16*(2), 122–131.

Barker, R. A. (2001). The nature of leadership. *Human Relations, 54*(4), 469–494.

Battilana, J., & Dorado, S. (2010). Building sustainable hybrid organizations: The case of commercial microfinance organizations. *Academy of Management Journal, 53*(6), 1419–1440.

Beck, A. P. (1981). A study of group phase development and emergent leadership. *Group, 5*(4), 48–54.

Bednarek, R., Paroutis, S., & Sillince, J. (2017). Transcendence through rhetorical practices: Responding to paradox in the science sector. *Organization Studies, 38*(1), 77–101.

Benner, M. J., & Tushman, M. L. (2003). Exploitation, exploration, and process management: The productivity dilemma revisited. *Academy of Management Review, 28*(2), 238–256.

Besharov, M. L. (2014). The relational ecology of identification: How organizational identification emerges when individuals hold divergent values. *Academy of Management Journal, 57*(5), 1485–1512.

Boeker, W., & Wiltbank, R. (2005). New venture evolution and managerial capabilities. *Organization Science, 16*(2), 123–133.

Bolden, R. (2011). Distributed leadership in organizations: A review of theory and research. *International Journal of Management Reviews, 13*(3), 251–269.

Carland, J. W., Hoy, F., Boulton, W. R., & Carland, J. A. C. (1984). Differentiating entrepreneurs from small business owners: A conceptualization. *Academy of Management Review, 9*(2), 354–359.

Casson, M. (2000). *Enterprise and leadership: Studies on firms, markets, and networks.* Cheltenham: Edward Elgar Publishing.

Coad, A., Cowling, M., & Siepel, J. (2017). Growth processes of high-growth firms as a four-dimensional chicken and egg. *Industrial and Corporate Change, 26*, 537–554.

Cope, J., Kempster, S., & Parry, K. (2011). Exploring distributed leadership in the small business context. *International Journal of Management Reviews, 13*(3), 270–285.

Cornelissen, J. P., Mantere, S., & Vaara, E. (2014). The contraction of meaning: The combined effect of communication, emotions, and materiality on sensemaking in the Stockwell shooting. *Journal of Management Studies, 51*(5), 699–735.

Cuganesan, S. (2017). Identity paradoxes: How senior managers and employees negotiate similarity and distinctiveness tensions over time. *Organization Studies, 38*(3–4), 489–511.

d'Amboise, G., & Muldowney, M. (1988). Management theory for small business: Attempts and requirements. *Academy of Management Review, 13*(2), 226–240.

Denis, J. L., Lamothe, L., & Langley, A. (2001). The dynamics of collective leadership and strategic change in pluralistic organizations. *Academy of Management Journal, 44*(4), 809–837.

DeSantola, A., & Gulati, R. (2017). Scaling: Organizing and growth in entrepreneurial ventures. Academy of Management Annals, *11*(2), 640–668.

Drazin, R., & Sandelands, L. (1992). Autogenesis: A perspective on the process of organizing. *Organization Science, 3*(2), 230–249.

Ensley, M. D., Hmieleski, K. M., & Pearce, C. L. (2006). The importance of vertical and shared leadership within new venture top management teams: Implications for the performance of startups. *The Leadership Quarterly, 17*(3), 217–231.

Ensley, M. D., Pearson, A., & Pearce, C. L. (2003). Top management team process, shared leadership, and new venture performance: A theoretical model and research agenda. *Human Resource Management Review, 13*(2), 329–346.

Fayol, H. (1949). General and industrial management. London: Sir Isaac Pitman & Sons Ltd.

Gehman, J., Treviño, L. K., & Garud, R. (2013). Values work: A process study of the emergence and performance of organizational values practices. *Academy of Management Journal, 56*(1), 84–112.

Gimmon, E. (2008). Entrepreneurial team-starts and teamwork: Taking the investors' perspective. *Team Performance Management: An International Journal, 14*(7/8), 327–339.

Greiner, L. E. (1989). *Evolution and revolution as organizations grow* (pp. 373–387). London: Macmillan Education UK.

Hahn, T., Preuss, L., Pinkse, J., & Figge, F. (2014). Cognitive frames in corporate sustainability: Managerial sensemaking with paradoxical and business case frames. *Academy of Management Review, 39*(4), 463–487.

Hargrave, T. J., & Van de Ven, A. H. (2017). Integrating dialectical and paradox perspectives on managing contradictions in organizations. *Organization Studies, 38*(3–4), 319–339.

Harper, D. A. (2008). Towards a theory of entrepreneurial teams. *Journal of Business Venturing, 23*(6), 613–626.

Heavey, C., & Simsek, Z. (2017). Distributed cognition in top management teams and organizational ambidexterity: The influence of transactive memory systems. *Journal of Management, 43*(3), 919–945.

Heenan, D. A., & Bennis, W. G. (1999). *Co-leaders: The power of great partnerships.* Texas: University of Texas Press.

Hitt, M. A., Ireland, R. D., Sirmon, D. G., & Trahms, C. A. (2011). Strategic entrepreneurship: Creating value for individuals, organizations, and society. *Academy of Management Perspectives, 25*(2), 57–75.

Hmieleski, K. M., & Ensley, M. D. (2007). A contextual examination of new venture performance: Entrepreneur leadership behavior, top management team heterogeneity, and environmental dynamism. *Journal of Organizational Behavior: The International Journal of Industrial, Occupational and Organizational Psychology and Behavior, 28*(7), 865–889.

Hogg, M. A., & Terry, D. I. (2000). Social identity and self-categorization processes in organizational contexts. *Academy of Management Review, 25*(1), 121–140.

Hosking, D. M. (1988). Organizing, leadership and skilful process. *Journal of Management Studies, 25*(2), 147–166.

Hunter, S. T., Cushenbery, L. D., & Jayne, B. (2017). Why dual leaders will drive innovation: Resolving the exploration and exploitation dilemma with a conservation of resources solution. *Journal of Organizational Behavior, 38*(8), 1183–1195.

Huq, J. L., Reay, T., & Chreim, S. (2017). Protecting the paradox of interprofessional collaboration. *Organization Studies, 38*(3–4), 513–538.

Jansen, J. J., George, G., Van den Bosch, F. A., & Volberda, H. W. (2008). Senior team attributes and organizational ambidexterity: The moderating role of transformational leadership. *Journal of Management Studies, 45*(5), 982–1007.

Jansen, J. J., Vera, D., & Crossan, M. (2009). Strategic leadership for exploration and exploitation: The moderating role of environmental dynamism. *The Leadership Quarterly, 20*(1), 5–18.

Jansen, J. J. P., & Roelofsen, O. (2018). *Focus today on the growth of tomorrow.* Whitepaper. Nlgroeit, March.

Jarzabkowski, P., Lê, J. K., & Van de Ven, A. H. (2013). Responding to competing strategic demands: How organizing, belonging, and performing paradoxes coevolve. *Strategic Organization, 11*(3), 245–280.

Jay, J. (2013). Navigating paradox as a mechanism of change and innovation in hybrid organizations. *Academy of Management Journal, 56*(1), 137–159.

Josefy, M., Kuban, S., Ireland, R. D., & Hitt, M. A. (2015). All things great and small: Organizational size, boundaries of the firm, and a changing environment. *Academy of Management Annals, 9*(1), 715–802.

Knight, D., Pearce, C. L., Smith, K. G., Olian, J. D., Sims, H. P., Smith, K. A., & Flood, P. (1999). Top management team diversity, group process, and strategic consensus. *Strategic Management Journal, 20*(5), 445–465.

Knight, E., & Cuganesan, S. (2019). Organisation ambidexterity: Valuation practices and the senior leadership team. *Human Relations, 73*(2), 190–214.

Knight, E., & Harvey, W. (2015). Managing exploration and exploitation paradoxes in creative organisations. *Management Decision, 53*(4), 809–827.

Knight, E., & Paroutis, S. (2017). Becoming salient: The TMT leader's role in shaping the interpretive context of paradoxical tensions. *Organization Studies, 38*(3–4), 403–432.

Kornberger, M. (2017). The values of strategy: Valuation practices, rivalry and strategic agency. *Organization Studies, 38*(12), 1753–1773.

Lechler, T. (2001). Social interaction: A determinant of entrepreneurial team venture success. *Small Business Economics, 16*, 263–278.

Lewis, M. W. (2000). Exploring paradox: Toward a more comprehensive guide. *Academy of Management Review, 25*(4), 760–776.

Lewis, R. (2010). *When cultures collide* (pp. 171–211). London: Nicholas Brealey Publishing.

Locke, E. (2003). Leadership: Starting at the top. In C. L. Pearce & J. A. Conger (Eds.), *Shared Leadership* (pp. 271–284). Thousand Oaks: Sage.

Lukoschek, C. S., Gerlach, G., Stock, R. M., & Xin, K. (2018). Leading to sustainable organizational unit performance: Antecedents and outcomes of executives' dual innovation leadership. *Journal of Business Research, 91*, 266–276.

Lüscher, L. S., & Lewis, M. W. (2008). Organizational change and managerial sensemaking: Working through paradox. *Academy of Management Journal, 51*(2), 221–240.

March, J. G. (1991). Exploration and exploitation in organizational learning. *Organization Science, 2*(1), 71–87.

Mintzberg, H. (1979). *The structuring of organizations*. Englewood Cliffs: Prentice Hall.

Mitchell, T. R., & James, L. R. (2001). Building better theory: Time and the specification of when things happen. *Academy of Management Review, 26*(4), 530–547.

Mom, T. J., Van Den Bosch, F. A., & Volberda, H. W. (2007). Investigating managers' exploration and exploitation activities: The influence of top-down, bottom-up, and horizontal knowledge inflows. *Journal of management studies, 44*(6), 910–931.

Morris, M. H., Zahra, S. A., & Schindehutte, M. (2000). Understanding factors that trigger entrepreneurial behavior in established companies. In Libecap, G.D. (Ed.) *Entrepreneurship and economic growth in the American economy* (pp. 133–159). Leeds: Emerald Group Publishing Limited.

Mueller, S., Chambers, L., & Neck, H. (2013). The distinctive skills of social entrepreneurs. *Journal of Enterprising Culture, 21*(03), 301–334.

Mumford, M. D., & Hunter, S. T. (2005). Innovation in organizations: A multi-level perspective on creativity. In M.D. Mumford, S.T Hunter, K.E. Bedell0-Avers, F.J. Yammarino, & F. Dansereau, *Multi-level issues in strategy and methods* (Vol. 4, pp. 9–73). Bingley: Emerald Group Publishing Limited.

Naffziger, D. W., Hornsby, J. S., & Kuratko, D. F. (1994). A proposed research model of entrepreneurial motivation. *Entrepreneurship Theory and Practice, 18*(3), 29–42.

Nicholls-Nixon, C. L. (2005). Rapid growth and high performance: The entrepreneur's "impossible dream?" *Academy of Management Perspectives, 19*(1), 77–89.

O'Reilly III, C. A., & Tushman, M. L. (2004). The ambidextrous organization. *Harvard Business Review, 82*(4), 74.

O'Reilly III, C. A., & Tushman, M. L. (2013). Organizational ambidexterity: Past, present, and future. *Academy of Management Perspectives, 27*(4), 324–338.

Orton, J. D., & Weick, K. E. (1990). Loosely coupled systems: A reconceptualization. *Academy of Management Review, 15*(2), 203–223.

Papachroni, A., Heracleous, L., & Paroutis, S. (2016). In pursuit of ambidexterity: Managerial reactions to innovation–efficiency tensions. *Human Relations, 29*(9), 1791–1822.

Pearce, C. L., & Conger, J. A. (2003). *Shared leadership: Reframing the hows and whys of leadership*. Thousand Oaks: Sage Publications.

Pearce, C. L., Conger, J. A., & Locke, E. A. (2007). Shared leadership theory. *The Leadership Quarterly, 18*(3), 281–288.

Pfeffer, J. (1994). Competitive advantage through people. *California Management Review, 36*(2), 9–28.

Ping, G., Feng, W., & Yanyan, Z. (2016, November). A review of enterprise top management team and organizational innovation. In *International Conference on Innovation and Management* (Vol. 13).

Poole, M. S., & Van de Ven, A. H. (1989). Using paradox to build management and organization theories. *Academy of management review, 14*(4), 562–578.

Poole, M. S., & Van de Ven, A. H. (Eds.) (2004). *Handbook of organizational change and innovation*. New York: Oxford University Press.

Pratt, M. G., & Rafaeli, A. (1997). Organizational dress as a symbol of multilayered social identities. *Academy of Management Journal, 40*(4), 862–898.

Probst, G., Raisch, S., & Tushman, M. L. (2011). Ambidextrous leadership: Emerging challenges for business and HR leaders. *Organizational Dynamics, 40*(4), 326–334.

116   *New thinking in action*

Raisch, S., & Birkinshaw, J. (2008). Organizational ambidexterity: Antecedents, outcomes, and moderators. *Journal of Management, 34*(3), 375–409.

Ray, G., Barney, J. B., & Muhanna, W. A. (2004). Capabilities, business processes, and competitive advantage: choosing the dependent variable in empirical tests of the resource-based view. *Strategic Management Journal, 25*(1), 23–37.

Reid, W., & Karambayya, R. (2009). Impact of dual executive leadership dynamics in creative organizations. *Human Relations, 62*(7), 1073–1112.

Rosenthal, C. S. (1998). Determinants of collaborative leadership: Civic engagement, gender or organizational norms? *Political Research Quarterly, 51*(4), 847–868.

Rosing, K., Frese, M., & Bausch, A. (2011). Explaining the heterogeneity of the leadership-innovation relationship: Ambidextrous leadership. *The Leadership Quarterly, 22*(5), 956–974.

Schumpeter, J. A. (1934). *The theory of economic development.* Cambridge: Harvard University Press.

Sheep, M. L., Fairhurst, G. T., & Khazanchi, S. (2017). Knots in the discourse of innovation: Investigating multiple tensions in a reacquired spin-off. *Organization Studies, 38*(3–4), 463–488.

Simons, T., Pelled, L. H., & Smith, K. A. (1999). Making use of difference: Diversity, debate, and decision comprehensiveness in top management teams. *Academy of Management Journal, 42*(6), 662–673.

Simsek, Z., Jansen, J. J., Minichilli, A., & Escriba-Esteve, A. (2015). Strategic leadership and leaders in entrepreneurial contexts: A nexus for innovation and impact missed? *Journal of Management Studies, 52*(4), 463–478.

Smith, W. K., Erez, M., Jarvenpaa, S., Lewis, M. W., & Tracey, P. (2017). Adding complexity to theories of paradox, tensions, and dualities of innovation and change: Introduction to organization studies special issue on paradox, tensions, and dualities of innovation and change. *Organization Studies, 38*(3–4), 303–317.

Smith, W. K., & Lewis, M. W. (2011). Toward a theory of paradox: A dynamic equilibrium model of organizing. *Academy of Management Review, 36*(2), 381–403.

Smith, W. K., & Tushman, M. L. (2005). Managing strategic contradictions: A top management model for managing innovation streams. *Organization Science, 16*(5), 522–536.

Stacey, R. D. (1995). The science of complexity: An alternative perspective for strategic change processes. *Strategic Management Journal, 16*(6), 477–495.

Stanford, N. (2007). *Guide to organisation design: Creating high-performing and adaptable enterprises* (Vol. 10). London: John Wiley & Sons.

Tajfel, H. (1982). Social psychology of intergroup relations. *Annual Review of Psychology, 33,* 1–39.

Tracey, P., Phillips, N., & Jarvis, O. (2011). Bridging institutional entrepreneurship and the creation of new organizational forms: A multilevel model. *Organization Science, 22*(1), 60–80.

Tracy, S. J. (2004). Dialectic, contradiction, or double bind? Analyzing and theorizing employee reactions to organizational tension. *Journal of Applied Communication Research, 32*(2), 119–146.

Tushman, M. L., & O'Reilly III, C. A. (1996). Ambidextrous organizations: Managing evolutionary and revolutionary change. *California Management Review, 38*(4), 8–29.

Vyakarnam, S., & Handelberg, J. (2005). Four themes of the impact of management teams on organizational performance: Implications for future research of entrepreneurial teams. *International Small Business Journal, 23*(3), 236–256.

Wasserman, N. (2003). Founder-CEO succession and the paradox of entrepreneurial success. *Organization Science, 14*(2), 149–172.

Watzlawick, P., Beavin, J., & Jackson, D. D. (1967). *Pragmatics of human communication: A study of interactional patterns, pathologies and paradoxes.* New York: W.W. Norton & Co.

Zahra, S. A., Sapienza, H. J., & Davidsson, P. (2006). Entrepreneurship and dynamic capabilities: A review, model and research agenda. *Journal of Management Studies, 43*(4), 917–955.

Zimmermann, A., Raisch, S., & Cardinal, L. B. (2018). Managing persistent tensions on the frontline: A configurational perspective on ambidexterity. *Journal of Management Studies, 55*(5), 739–769.

6   Conclusion

As organisations innovate and grow, they experience significant tensions from competing demands, and senior leaders are expected to 'recognise and translate different, ambiguous, and conflicting expectations into workable strategies'.[1]

Encouraging senior leaders to work as a team is recognised as an important mechanism by which team effectiveness can be enhanced in organisations facing these competing demands.[2] Although there has been significant interest in the literature on the different types of paradoxical tensions senior leaders experience in these contexts, investigations into how these tensions are experienced and addressed by the senior leadership team as a whole have only been relatively recent. Few studies have explored how individual senior leaders' behaviours and cognitive frames come together for senior leadership teams to reach shared consensus as a team.[3]

This study reveals the collective sensemaking practices of senior leadership teams seeking to innovate for-purpose. The findings provide contributions to the literature on sensemaking, leadership, and paradox. Some key findings include: identifying how rapid change contexts can generate paradoxical tensions; moving beyond the single entrepreneurial leader to distributed leadership models that can address the polar tensions; valuing strategic sensemaking for simultaneous paradox management; and recognising the power of an integrated core purpose.

Despite the recognised tendency for leadership teams to seek alignment for cohesive action,[4] this research identified how sustainable alignment is only possible where there is a practical enactment of paradoxical sensemaking practices. This empowers all team members and enables opposing orientations to coexist in synergy. The 'purpose-driven' mission of the organisation can in effect lead to destructive tensions and greater dissent for a senior leadership team where there is no clear strategic direction that integrates the different orientations to competing demands.

Integrated alignment will require a recognition of the paradoxical nature of the different sensemaking orientations. It will also require an understanding of how the innovation orientations of both 'exploration' and 'exploitation' can work together in synergy to contribute to the fulfilment of the organisation

DOI: 10.4324/9781003426691-6

values and purpose. This new 'ambidextrous' way of working can aid the development of a strong collaborative alignment in a senior leadership team.

The research identified that there are two clear requirements for a senior leadership team to reach strategic alignment. Firstly, important shifts from *divergence to validation and integration* can be enabled through collective sensemaking. In order to transition from survival and chaos, as represented by divergent individual positions, to thriving as a senior leadership team and as an organisation, it is important to go through a phase of validation through paradoxical awareness. This, in turn, will enable integration in alignment and greater consensus in strategic focus. A shift from *divergence to validation* is facilitated by the senior leadership team collectively embracing and embodying paradoxical principles. A shift from *validation to integration* is then facilitated through the development of a shared integrated narrative that actively incorporates these paradoxical principles and enables alignment.

Where senior leaders take dual roles in teams they can construct multiple narratives.[5] This research also demonstrates how a strong single vision can enable the integration of different orientations within a team. This is consistent with the literature on identification and how a shared story can help to foster shared purpose,[6] yet the findings of this study also provide further insight into the need for intentional strategies that can be adapted by an organisation in identity transition.

Collective sensemaking functions as a form of social discourse that brings together divergent individual cognitive perspectives and strategic concerns. For this to occur effectively, at least some members of the team need to recognise and make sense of the paradoxical nature of competing demands to move from divergent individual positions to the validation of oppositional orientations. The research findings outlined in this book demonstrate that an awareness of the competing demands – otherwise known as 'paradoxical cognition'–helps individuals to manage these tensions more effectively. This phenomenon was not only evident at the individual level, but it was also identified that leadership units can also activate collective paradoxical cognition, even where there is only partial individual-level paradoxical cognition. This research therefore provides a valuable contribution to the sensemaking literature by demonstrating how this collective sensemaking process can enable these shifts and by identifying in granular detail the principles and practices behind how the senior leadership team collective sensemaking process operates when dealing with competing demands in innovation contexts.[7]

The research also makes a contribution to the paradox literature by demonstrating how a senior leadership team can achieve alignment from divergent polar positions related to innovation. An integrated concept or story that incorporates the value of both orientations simultaneously can serve as a mutually accepted validation of the paradoxical orientations represented and can then enable strategic focus and action. Where a senior leadership team responds effectively to the tensions generated by the competing demands, they will be able to maximise the potential of a clear core purpose to propel the organisation forward for effective innovation and growth – rather than becoming victim to the potential destructive nature of these tensions.

As not-for-profits and social entrepreneurs are more likely to be driven by for-purpose values,[8] which was identified in this case, these values can provide a strong magnetic force to hold opposing elements together in alignment. Further, as an association was found between a senior team shared vision and an organisation's ability to deal with the paradoxical demands of innovation and growth,[9] this research reinforces that alignment around a core purpose can provide a cohesive compelling force to hold divergent elements from competing demands together in dynamic tension and prevent fragmentation.[10] Where the core purpose is represented by an integrated story or metaphor, the relatedness of paradoxical orientations can become more salient to organisation actors and can enable a senior leadership team to find points of connection for strategic alignment.

An additional overarching contribution to paradox theory emerged from the finding that polar positions from competing demands can only be sustained as 'independent yet interdependent' paradox pairs where there is an awareness of the relational binding force (core purpose) that can hold these paradoxical polar positions in tension. This can have a commanding unifying power for a senior leadership team by helping to surface the paradoxical nature of competing demands predominantly where paradoxical elements are identified, clarified and affirmed by at least some members of the team.

The physics concept of 'magnetic forces' was introduced as an illustrative metaphor to demonstrate how the core values and purpose can act as an invisible magnetic field that connects paradoxical polar positions. The core purpose also ensures both polar positions do not drift too far apart. This involves accepting the idea that paradoxical positions are necessarily both independent and interdependent, complementary and contradictory. The findings of this study therefore demonstrate how consensus can be reached for senior leadership teams facing competing demands as they innovate and grow where collective sensemaking shifts have been enabled, and where there is shared integrated alignment around a core purpose.

As this research is a single case study, observations need to be made in other organisations in other contexts to identify common experiences and patterns and provide further insight into the related phenomena. Nevertheless, the findings contribute to the theoretical understanding of how leaders make sense of and respond to competing innovation demands in senior leadership teams, and also provide practical implications for practice by demonstrating how senior team alignment around competing demands can be achieved.

It is my hope that this work will provide helpful insights to activate purpose-driven innovation leadership for sustainable development in a range of contexts.

Notes

1 Jansen et al., 2008, p. 985
2 Jansen et al., 2008
3 Hargrave and Van De Ven, 2017
4 O'Leary and Williams, 2012, Van der Hoorn and Whitty, 2017
5 Balogun, Bartunek and Do, 2015
6 Brown, Stacey and Nandhakumar, 2008
7 Brown, Stacey and Nandhakumar, 2008, Donnellon, Gray and Bougon, 1986, Weick, 1979, 1995
8 Parrish, 2010
9 Jansen et al., 2008
10 Hambrick, 1994, Orton and Weick, 1990, Ouchi, 2019

References

Balogun, J., Bartunek, J. M., & Do, B. (2015). Senior managers' sensemaking and responses to strategic change. *Organization Science, 26*(4), 960–979.

Brown, A. D., Stacey, P., & Nandhakumar, J. (2008). Making sense of sensemaking narratives. *Human Relations, 61*(8), 1035–1062.

Donnellon, A., Gray, B., & Bougon, M. G. (1986). Communication, meaning, and organized action. *Administrative Science Quarterly, 31*(1), 43–55.

Hambrick, Donald C. (1994). Top management groups: A conceptual integration and reconsideration of the 'team' label. In B. M. Staw & L. L. Cummings (Eds.), *Research in Organizational Behavior, 16*, 171–214. Greenwich, CT: JAI Press.

Hargrave, T. J., & Van de Ven, A. H. (2017). Integrating dialectical and paradox perspectives on managing contradictions in organizations. *Organization Studies, 38*(3–4), 319–339.

Jansen, J. J., George, G., Van den Bosch, F. A., & Volberda, H. W. (2008). Senior team attributes and organizational ambidexterity: The moderating role of transformational leadership. *Journal of Management Studies, 45*(5), 982–1007.

O'Leary, T., & Williams, T. (2012). Managing the social trajectory: A practice perspective on project management. *IEEE Transactions on Engineering Management, 60*(3), 566–580.

Orton, J. D., & Weick, K. E. (1990). Loosely coupled systems: A reconceptualization. *Academy of Management Review, 15*(2), 203–223.

Ouchi, W. G. (2019). Markets, bureaucracies, and clans. In A. J. Berry, J. Broadbent, and D. T. Otley *Management Control Theory* (pp. 343–356). Abingdon: Routledge.

Parrish, B. D. (2010). Sustainability-driven entrepreneurship: Principles of organization design. *Journal of Business Venturing, 25*(5), 510–523.

Van der Hoorn, B., & Whitty, S. J. (2017). The praxis of 'alignment seeking' in project work. *International Journal of Project Management, 35*(6), 978–993.

Weick, K. E. (1979). *The social psychology of organizing* (2nd ed.). New York: McGraw-Hill.

Weick, K. E. (1995). Sensemaking in Organisations. Thousand Oaks: Sage Publications.

Index